Anonymous

Abraham Lincoln and Reformers

Anonymous

Abraham Lincoln and Reformers

ISBN/EAN: 9783337296889

Printed in Europe, USA, Canada, Australia, Japan

Cover: Foto ©ninafisch / pixelio.de

More available books at **www.hansebooks.com**

Abraham Lincoln and Reformers

Frederick Douglass

Excerpts from newspapers and other sources

From the files of the

Lincoln Financial Foundation Collection

FREDERICK DOUGLASS AT MR. LINCOLN'S RECEPTION.

Mr. Lincoln personally invited Mr. Douglass to attend his first reception. He had been dissuaded from going by some friends after he had received the invitation. His friends of African descent who had promised to attend him did not go. Speaking of their decision, Mr. Douglass said:

"It was plainly quite the thing for me to attend President Lincoln's reception, 'they all with one accord, began to make excuse.' It was finally arranged that Mrs. Dorsey should bear me company; so, together, we joined in the great procession of citizens from all parts of the country, and moved slowly toward the executive mansion. I had, for some time, looked upon myself as a man, but now, in the multitude of the elite of the land, I felt myself a man among men. I regret to be obliged to say, however, that this comfortable assurance was not of long duration; for, on reaching the door, two policemen stationed there took me rudely by the arm and ordered me to stand back—their orders were to admit no persons of my color. The reader need not be told that this was a disagreeable setback. But once in the battle, I did not think it well to submit to a repulse. I told the officers I was quite sure there must be some mistake, for no such order could have emanated from President Lincoln, and if he knew I was at the door he would desire my admission. They then, to put an end to the parley, as I suppose—for we were obstructing the doorway, and were not easily pushed aside—assumed an air of politeness and offered to conduct me in. We followed their lead, and soon found ourselves walking some planks out of a window, which had been arranged as a temporary passage for the exit of visitors. We halted, so soon as we saw the trick, and I said to the officers: 'You deceived me. I shall not go out of this building till I see President Lincoln.' At this moment a gentleman who was passing in recognized me, and I said to him: 'Be so kind as to say to Mr. Lincoln that Frederick Douglass is detained by officers at the door.' It was not long before Mrs. Dorsey and I walked into the spacious east room, amid a scene of elegance such as, in this country, I had never witnessed before. Like a mountain pine, high above all others, Mr. Lincoln stood, in his grand simplicity and homelike beauty. Recognizing me, even before I reached him, he exclaimed, so that all around could hear him, 'Here comes my friend Douglass!' Taking me by the hand, he said: 'I am glad to see you. I saw you in the crowd to-day, listening to my inaugural address. How did you like it?' I said: 'Mr. Lincoln, I must not detain you with my poor opinion, when there are thousands waiting to shake hands with you.' 'No! no!' he said; 'you must stop a little, Douglass. There is no man in the country whose opinion I value more than yours. I want to know what you think of it?' I replied, 'Mr. Lincoln, that was a sacred effort.' 'I am glad you liked it!' he said, and I passed on, feeling that any man, however distinguished, might well regard himself honored by such expressions from such a man.

"It came out that the officers at the White House had received no orders from Mr. Lincoln, or from anyone else. They were simply complying with an old custom, the outgrowth of slavery, as dogs will sometimes rub their necks long after the collars are removed, thinking they are still there. My colored friends were well pleased with what had seemed to them a doubtful experiment, and I believe were encouraged by its success to follow my example. I have found in my experience that the way to break down an unreasonable custom is to contradict it in practice."

ing, it 1897

SOME PERSONAL RECOLLECTIONS

DR. BLAKESLEE ON DOUGLASS.

From an Address Given in Los Angeles, Calif.

Considering the depths from which he came and the heights to which he climbed, the achievements of Frederick Douglass can scarcely be equalled in all the records of mankind. Born of a slave mother whom he never even saw but a very few times and who died when he was but eight years old, and of an unknown white father, he ran an amazing career in the most crucial period of our national history and died lamented by two continents and enshrined forever in the hearts of millions of adoring friends.

From the blighting surroundings of a slave plantation, from depths of ignorance and debasement paralleled only in a land of cannibals, Frederick Douglass made his dramatic escape and by prodigious effort at self culture rose to be the equal, often the superior, of the great men and superb orators of his time.

To escape arrest and return to bondage he fled to England where, and in Ireland and Scotland, for two years he associated with the leading statesmen of those lands. They called him the "Black O'Connell." He there espoused not only American emancipation but temperance, peace and greater freedom for the people in several of their national issues. Friends in England raised the money which bo't his freedom. His last night abroad was as a guest of John Bright.

In this country he was the associate on the platform and often in the home of such as Charles Sumner, Wendell Phillips, Wm. Lloyd Garrison, Ralph Waldo Emerson, and a score of others. He was called in conference by Abraham Lincoln who invited him to dine with him. He was the United States Minister to the Republic of Hayti, elector-at-Large of the State of New York at the second election of General Grant, and was chosen by the electors to carry the result to Washington; he was president of the Freedmen's Bank at Washington, Member of the San Domingo Commission, member of the upper house of the Legislature of the District of Columbia, United States Marshal of the same, agent for Hayti at the World's Columbian Exposition at Chicago, Registrar of Deeds for the District of Columbia under three Presidents, besides editor for years of journals in the interest of the negro race, and last but not lease he was for a time a Methodist local preacher.

He was bold almost to rashness in his anti-slavery work, often suffering violence. A mob in Indiana clubbed him into insensibility and left him for dead. But like the Apostle Paul he could say, "None of these things move me neither count I my life dear unto myself if by any means I may help win the freedom of my people."

His bronze statue, which I have often seen, stands in a conspicuous spot in the city of Rochester, N. Y., where he lived many years, and his bust in the library of the college in the same city.

But I was asked to speak on personal recollections of Frederick Douglass. My first recollection was hearing him speak in Washington, where I was a clerk in the Quartermaster General's office, August 18, 1864. It was the evening of the day that I had called on the Assistant Secretary of War, Charles A. Dana, who afterward for a generation was the master of American journalism as editor of the New York Sun. The subject and the circumstances of the Douglass address I have forgotten. Did you get it? August 18, 1864. There was then a well nigh panic among loyal citizens over the probable defeat at the approaching November election of Abraham Lincoln for his second term. Leonard Swett wrote: "Unless material changes can be wrought Lincoln's election is beyond any possible hope. It is probably clean gone now." It was five days only before Lincoln himself wrote: "It seems exceedingly probable that this administration will not be re-elected."

In last January's Atlantic Monthly there is an account of the founding at Washington of a lecture course, the main object of which was to offset disloyal influences and sustain the administration in its efforts to bring victory to our armies and to restore the Union. Among other speakers were Horace Greely, Gerritt Smith, Ralph Waldo Emerson, Wendell Phillips, Frederick Douglass. It is quite probable that this speech to which I listened was in the interest of Lincoln's re-election, which Douglass and the anti-slavery leaders considered so essential to the total destruction of slavery and the salvation of the nation. In his autobiography Douglass says: "I certainly exerted myself to the utmost to secure his re-election."

Fred Douglass' personal appearance was Websterian. Over six feet and proportionately well built, and straight as an arrow, musular yet lithe and graceful, with a wealth of bushy hair, in later years a silver crown of glory, a voice musical, full and sonorous in the depth and richness of its cadences, he stood the embodiment of majestic, terrifying power, the dusky Ajax, as he hurled his lightning flashes against that inhuman system which had enchained his race for two hundred fifty years.

Frederick Douglass married for his second wife a white woman, Miss Helen Pitts, from one of the best families of Western New York. This occasioned considerable criticism from both blacks and whites. In a public address, when the feeling was intense he said: "My first wife was the color of my mother, and my second wife the color of my father; you see I wanted to be perfectly fair to both races." The second Mrs. Douglass had relatives at East Greenwich, R. I., where I was principal of the East Greenwich Academy. She and her husband came in the 90's to visit these relatives. I called upon them and engaged Mr. Douglass to address my students. In introducing him I said to the students:

"I want to present to you two pictures. The first is in a Maryland jail. A slave boy arrested in his attempt to escape from his master stands manacled. Outside are jeering slave dealers ready to start with him in the morning for the canebrakes of Louisiana where a slave's life averages four years. My second picture is at the capital of the nation. The occasion the unvailing of a statue of the great emancipator, Abraham Lincoln, the gift of the freedmen of America. The audience one of the most august assemblies of earth; General Grant, then President of the United States, his cabinet, the United States Senate, members of the House of Representatives, the Supreme Court, and many other high officials and illustrious citizens. The orator, the slave boy in my first picture whom I am happy to present to you today. Can you match that story in all the annals of time? And by the way, General Grant said of this address of

Frederick Douglass that it was the best analysis of the character and career of Abraham Lincoln to which he had ever listened. I could hardly have brought to my young people any other in all this broad land who was so inspiring an example of what a youth in this country, however handicapped, may become, in this country, which largely due to the labor of Frederick Douglass, had then become more truly the land of opportunity, the land of the free and the home of the brave.

Paraphrasing somewhat the utterances of Wendell Phillips concerning another black hero: "I would call Frederick Douglass Napoleon, but Napoleon won by broken promises and seas of blood. This man was the soul of honor. I would call him Cromwell, but Cromwell was only a soldier. This man must be classed with America's greatest statesmen. I would call him Washington, but the great Virginian held slaves. This man was himself a slave and none of his generation struck sturdier blows against this 'sum of all villainies.'" Possibly some of you may think me a fanatic tonight as I plead, as did he, for equal rights for all in the name of Him who made of one blood all nations of men to dwell on all the face of the earth, knowing no distinction of race, or color, or tongue, or clime, for all are brothers. If any of you thus think you have read history not with your eyes but with your prejudices. Fifty, perhaps hundred of years hence, when Truth gets a full hearing, when the teachings of the Galilean shall have universal sway, the Muse of History will put Phocian for the Greek, Brutus for the Roman, Hampden for England, LaFayette for France, choose Washington as the bright consummate flower of our earlier civilization, Abraham Lincoln the ripe fruit of our noonday, then, dipping her pen in the sunlight will write in the clear blue, in the galaxy of world immortals, the name of the Christian here, the unfaltering patriot, the suffering martyr, the paragon of his race, Frederick Douglass.

Dictionary of
American Negro
Biography

EDITED BY

Rayford W. Logan

AND

Michael R. Winston

W · W · NORTON & COMPANY

NEW YORK · LONDON

near present-day Bismarck, N.D., and supported his wife by cutting wood for the fort. In early fall of 1865 he was hired for that chore by the trading firm of Durfee and Peck.

On Nov. 11, 1865, according to military records, Dorman was hired by Lt. James M. Marshall of the 13th Infantry to carry the mail between Fort Rice and Fort Wadsworth. He made the 360-mile round trip only once that year but his reputation for diligence and dependability was established. Between 1865 and 1876 he rendered valuable service to the army in various capacities, among them a stint as guide and interpreter for the Northern Pacific Railroad survey of 1871. During this period his average earnings from governmental sources were about $60 per month, a goodly sum during those years. On Oct. 19, 1871, the commanding general of the Military Department of the Dakotas, in Special Order No. 149, hired Dorman to serve as post interpreter at Fort Rice at the rate of $75 per month. His skill with the Sioux language and an apparent understanding of the problems of both red and white men helped avert many "incidents" at Fort Rice. An easygoing manner and the strong smoking and chewing tobacco of which he was inordinately fond, and which he readily shared with his Indian friends, brought many of the hostiles to the fort in friendly trading visits.

Dorman's immediate superior was Lt. William Van Horne of the 17th Infantry. In 1872 Van Horne was transferred and Dorman served under Capt. James Wall Scully of the Quartermaster Corps until he served with General Custer and the 7th Cavalry. Custer was noted for his desire to have only the best available in his selection of civilian employees to accompany his expeditions. He knew of Dorman's prowess, and when preparing for the 1876 summer expedition against hostile and recalcitrant Indians, caused Special Order No. 2 (May 14, 1876) to be issued. "The commanding officer Ft. Rice, D.T. [Dakota Territory] will order Isaiah Dorman, Post interpreter to proceed to this post and report for duty to accompany the expedition as Interpreter—During his absence he will still be borne on the rolls of the Post Quartermaster at Fort Rice." Dorman was officially hired as interpreter by the 7th Cavalry by the regimental quartermaster, Lt. Henri J. Nowlan, and assumed duties on May 15, 1876, at the pay rate of $75 per month.

Custer's command arrived at the "Crow's Nest," an Indian landmark about fifteen miles east of the Little Bighorn River on June 25, 1876. It was there that Custer made the controversial division of his command. Dorman, as did most of the civilian employees, accompanied Maj. Marcus A. Reno's battalion of three companies. This arm of the assault crossed the Little Bighorn and executed an abortive attack on the southern perimeter of the hostile village. A skirmish line was formed, but after a few minutes Major Reno ordered a retreat to the timber bordering the west bank of the river. It was at the edge of this timber that, early in the fight, Isaiah Dorman received a fatal chest wound from the rifle of an Indian marksman. Unable to mount or ride a horse, Dorman, with several others, including famed scout "Lonesome Charley" Reynolds, was left to the dubious mercy of the Sioux. Reports as to atrocities committed

upon his body are varied but one enlisted man on the burial detail reported that when Dorman's body was found, it had been stripped, more than a dozen arrows shot into his chest, and a cavalry picket-pin driven through his genitals.

At the time of his demise $102.50 was due him for services during the months of May and June. The money was never rightfully claimed and remains unpaid. In all probability he died without issue. Fort Rice medical records fail to disclose any pregnancy or childbirth in his wife's name.

In his report of the battle Major Reno made the only reference to the color of Isaiah's skin. He also omitted his surname in his casualty report. Someone, at a later date, penciled "Dorman" beside the major's entry. That sparse entry is followed by the words "Killed by Indians."

Roland C. McConnell's "Isaiah Dorman and the Custer Expedition" UNH, July 1948, pp. 344–52) and Robert J. Ege's "Custer's Negro Interpreter" (Black World, Feb. 1965, pp. 29–35) give essential details; see also Edward C. Campbell's "Saving the Custer Muster Rolls" (Military Affairs, Summer 1946). The following records in the National Archives are essential: Medical History of Fort Rice, 1865–1876, Quartermaster's Reports of Persons and Articles Hired, June 1876, Seventh U.S. Regiment of Cavalry; Register of Claims, 1877 and 1878, vol. 5, Quartermaster General's Office, M.A. Reno Report of Battle of the Little Big Horn . . . , Record Group 94. — ROBERT J. EGE

DOUGLASS, FREDERICK (1817–1895), orator, journalist, reformer, public servant, and often referred to as the "father of the civil rights movement." Douglass was born a slave in Tuckahoe, Md. Sent to Baltimore in 1825 to be a houseboy, he escaped thirteen years later and settled in New Bedford, Mass. A talent for public speaking led him into the organized abolitionist movement as an agent for the Massachusetts Anti-Slavery Society. In 1845 he published his Narrative of the Life of Frederick Douglass, the first and most important of three autobiographies. In 1847 he began a career in journalism, publishing and editing a reformist weekly. His spirits were braced by the Civil War, which he viewed as a golden opportunity to strike at slavery. He urged Negroes to join the Union Armies, himself becoming an official recruiter. During the Reconstruction period he resumed his reformist activities, including his demands that Negroes be given the ballot and their full civil rights. A staunch Republican, his party rewarded him with three appointive positions during the closing phases of his career.

The heights to which Douglass rose stood in sharp contrast to his obscure parentage and humble beginnings. Born a slave, Douglass never knew the date of his birth. He assumed that he was born in 1817 and he took February 14 as his birthday because his mother, Harriet Bailey, had referred to him as her valentine. His knowledge of his mother was, in his words, "very scanty." When he was eight or nine his mother died, having worked as a field slave on a plantation twelve miles distant from her son. Douglass's father was an even more shadowy figure, never emerging from anonymity.

although Douglass believed that he was white and possibly his master, Aaron Anthony.

Too young to work in the fields, Douglass did odd jobs and ran errands. A favorite companion of his master's son, he seldom felt the whip, suffering more from hunger and cold. In 1825 Douglass was sent to Baltimore, a turning point in his life. Here for eight years he served as a houseboy and an unskilled laborer and learned to read and write. Returned to the plantation in 1832, Douglass was dismayed by the restrictions of rural slavery that contrasted sharply with the more permissive life of the city. He made an attempt to escape, forging passes for himself and four comrades. The attempt was thwarted but instead of being branded on the forehead or sold to the lower South, Douglass was sent back to Baltimore. For the next two years he worked in the shipyards, becoming an expert caulker. Still bent on escaping, he succeeded in September 1838, impersonating a sailor whose papers he borrowed.

Upon his arrival in New York City Douglass had the good fortune to be directed to the secretary of the Negro-run New York Vigilance Committee, David Ruggles, who spent much of his time in assisting runaways. While under Ruggles's roof Douglass was married to Anna Murray, a Marylander whom he had met in Baltimore and who, herself free, had stimulated his desire to liberate himself. After the marriage the newlyweds went to New Bedford, Mass., where Douglass took the name by which he is known to history and where he worked at any job, however menial or low-paid, that became available. Color prejudice prevented Douglass from getting work as a ship caulker, but his race and previous condition of servitude opened to him an unexpected calling—abolitionist.

The organized movement to abolish slavery, which had gained new momentum in the 1830s, counted many Negro men and women among its supporters. Hence it is not surprising that within six months after Douglass arrived in New Bedford he became a regular reader of the militant weekly, the *Liberator*, and an admirer of its outspoken editor, William Lloyd Garrison of Boston. The personification of the uncompromising school of abolitionists, Garrison demanded that the slaves be freed immediately and without compensation to their masters. In August 1841 while attending an abolitionist gathering at Nantucket, Mass., with Garrison present, Douglass was unexpectedly called upon to speak. His words were halting, but as he spoke with feeling of his experiences in slavery the crowd listened attentively. Sensing his platform potentialities, the officers of the Massachusetts Anti-Slavery Society immediately urged him to become one of their agents. Refusing to take "no" for an answer, they prevailed upon Douglass to take a trial appointment of three months.

During the following four years the young ex-slave was one of the prize speakers of the society. Six feet tall and broad-shouldered, he had the build of an athlete. His deep-set eyes were steady and searching. His face was bronze-colored, with a thin line of black chin whiskers set off by a white cravat. He wore his hair long, a thick mass but freshly brushed as a rule and neatly parted on the left.

Often traveling in company with Wendell Phillips, the

prince of nineteenth-century orators, Douglass was not slow in developing his own speaking qualities. His voice, a rich and melodious baritone, was a flexible instrument, capable of varying degrees of light and shade. Newspaper editor N. P. Rogers, appraising him four months after he had become an abolitionist lecturer, found "his enunciation quite elegant," adding that "he has wit, argument, sarcasm and pathos."

The content of his addresses added to Douglass as a platform attraction. At first he was content to confine himself to a recital of his experiences in slavery. Gradually he broadened his scope, presenting the standard abolitionist arguments against slavery. But however familiar the theme, a speech by the maturing Douglass was carefully organized and equally reasoned. Although never speaking in public inadequately prepared, Douglass had the ability to think on his feet, particularly in responding to hecklers. Hence it is not surprising that sometimes his listeners wondered whether a man of such eloquence and platform poise could ever have been held in bondage. "People doubted if I had ever been a slave," he wrote in the second of his autobiographies. "They said I did not talk like a slave, look like a slave, nor act like a slave."

To prove that he was not an imposter Douglass published an account of his slave experiences, *Narrative of the Life of Frederick Douglass*, a slim volume of 125 pages, prefaced by letters from Garrison and Phillips. Appearing in May 1845, the book immediately became a bestseller in reformist circles. The work belonged to a distinctive genre, the "heroic fugitive" school of American literature. Designed as a plea for human freedom, the *Narrative* was much like its prototypes in its general approach—a succession of sorrowful stories couched in bitterly indignant tones. Douglass's *Narrative*, however, had special points of merit which would make it a landmark in the literary crusade against slavery.

To begin with, it came from the pen of Douglass himself rather than from that of a ghost-writer, as did many of the slave narratives. Thus by its very authorship it struck at the notion of Negro inferiority. Its literary qualities included pathos, such as in the passages on Douglass's mother, a reflective tone, such as his apostrophe to a ship's putting out to sea; and a sense of objectivity, such as its portrayal of certain all-too-human characteristics of the slaves themselves. The *Narrative*, moreover, had the great asset of credibility, giving specific names of persons and places. Indeed the credibility of his narrative exposed Douglass to the danger of being seized by his former master, now no longer in the dark as to his whereabouts. This sobering possibility gave the final impetus to his plans to tour the British Isles. With his book as a path-breaker he would have new audiences for the abolitionist message.

Arriving at Liverpool in August 1845 Douglass spent twenty-one months in England, Ireland, and Scotland, often traveling alone but sometimes in company with other reformers, British or American. His tour can justly be described as triumphal. As a rule his audiences were large and, even more invariably, sympathetic. The response he evoked against slavery would soon lead a score of other Negro reformers across the Atlantic, repeating his message and giving a new dimension to mid-Victorian humanitarianism. His cordial reception on the public platform was matched in other quarters. His personal treatment at hotels and inns was all he could have wished. He made the acquaintance of Parliamentary leaders Richard Cobden and John Bright, and had a dinner with the renowned abolitionist Thomas Clarkson. The many friends of Douglass raised money to purchase his freedom and upon his mention that he might like to edit a newspaper they gave him a purse of $2175 for the venture. Some of his new friends pleaded with Douglass to send for his wife and four children and take up permanent residence in the British Isles. But Douglass felt that his future was in his native land, to which he owed much—and vice versa.

Upon his return to America in August 1847 Douglass found that his Massachusetts friends, particularly William Lloyd Garrison, were cool toward his idea of starting a newspaper. For a year Douglass heeded their advice. But on Nov. 1, 1847, he moved his family to Rochester, N.Y., where five weeks later he brought out the first issue of the *North Star*, sharing for a time a joint editorship with Martin R. Delany, the founder-editor of the *Pittsburgh Mystery*. "Wielding my pen, as well as my voice" in the service of "my enslaved and oppressed people" was the reason Douglass gave for launching his weekly. Unquestionably, as he himself was quick to note, the publishing of a weekly brought him in much closer contact with the free black community than had been the case when he was an agent of an antislavery society. Upon becoming a journalist Douglass developed a deeper sense of identification with his Negro fellows, never seeking to deny his color or his kind. "Whatever character or capacity you ascribe to us, I am not ashamed to be numbered with this race," he said in May 1853 in an address to the American and Foreign Anti-Slavery Society. "I shall bring the Negro with me," he once wrote in response to an invitation to lecture.

A sense of racial pride led Douglass to advocate group solidarity and economic development and to condemn color prejudice and discrimination. Holding that blacks should unite for their advancement, Douglass inevitably became a major figure in the Colored Convention Movement, to give it the name by which it is known to history. Beginning in 1830 colored leaders throughout the North had held periodic meetings to make clear their attitude on public issues and to take concerted action thereon. At the meeting held in Cleveland in 1848, Douglass was chosen president. A year later Douglass proposed through the columns of the *North Star* that a new organization be formed, bearing the title "The National League" and with the motto "The union of the oppressed for the sake of freedom." The suggestion died aborning. Douglass did not permit his mortification to prevent him from playing an important role in subsequent colored conventions.

It is hardly surprising that Douglass gave much attention to the greatest hurdle facing the colored people in the North—job discrimination. He became one of the leading exponents of vocational education. "We need mechanics as well as ministers," he wrote in "Learn Trades or Starve," one of his most widely quoted

editorials. "We must build as well as live in houses; we must make as well as use furniture; we must construct bridges as well as pass over them."

Along with his emphasis on skilled labor, Douglass urged upon his fellow Negroes the standard virtues of middle-class morality—industry, thrift, honesty, and sobriety. The columns of his weekly sometimes read like a black *Poor Richard's Almanac.* But unlike a much later contemporary, Booker T. Washington, with whom he shared many economic viewpoints and character-building ideas, Douglass did not soft-pedal racial discrimination against blacks. He was unceasing in his condemnation of all forms of color prejudice. He challenged Jim Crow head-on, making it a practice to enter public places in which he might be coolly received if not summarily ejected.

Although proud of his color and bitter about discrimination against black people, Douglass was not antiwhite. By the time he joined the abolitionists his slavery-days distrust of whites had left him. He viewed whites as individuals, not stereotyping them. Douglass had a host of friends across the color line; perhaps no black leader was as relaxed as he in the presence of whites.

Douglass's broad sense of brotherhood led him to take an active role in reforms that were not primarily Negro-centered, among them temperance and women's rights. In the latter movement he was a pioneer. He was present at the meeting at Seneca Falls, N.Y., in July 1848 which formally inaugurated the women's rights movement in the United States. Besides giving a major address he was prominent in the session-to-session deliberations. He remained a staunch women's righter, a dependable supporter of the great triumvirate, Elizabeth Cady Stanton, Lucretia Mott, and Susan B. Anthony.

A man of many interests, a true reformer in the round, Douglass never forgot, however, that his main target was slavery. He spoke about it, he wrote about it, and he gave money to assist fugitives. His printing shop in Rochester was a station on the Underground Railroad. Over a ten-year span no fewer than 400 runaways found refuge under the Douglass roof, having received "food, shelter, counsel and comfort," before being sped on to nearby Canada.

Douglass shared the general abolitionist hostility to the Fugitive Slave Act of 1850, a measure that denied both the testimony of the alleged runaway and his right to a trial by jury. In the chorus of condemnation that followed, no language was stronger than that of Douglass. He told an audience in Boston's Faneuil Hall that if the law were put into operation the streets of the city would run with blood. He advised a Pittsburgh gathering that the way to make the Fugitive Slave Act a dead letter was to make some dead kidnappers. His weekly carried an editorial, "The True Remedy for the Fugitive Slave Bill," which turned out to be a "good revolver, a steady hand, and a determination to shoot down any man attempting to kidnap."

Many abolitionists, Douglass among them, reasoned that such a monstrosity as a fugitive slave law could never have been passed with the right kind of Congress. For nearly ten years Douglass believed that political action was the best way to strike at slavery. Shortly after

moving to Rochester he had become a voting abolitionist, prepared "to use the tense rhetoric of the ballot
box," as he put it. The Liberty party, born in 1840, had
practically run its course by the time Douglass became
a political activist, but in 1852 Douglass gave his support to its successor, the Free Soil party. In the presidential elections four years later Douglass supported the
new Republican party.

Douglass's venture into reform politics was unfruitful,
the growing rift between the North and South seeming
not to respond to peaceful approaches. The growing
sectional polarization was heightened by the Dred Scott
decision, which drew the Douglass ire because of its
ruling that Negroes were not citizens. The latent violence of the times was further fanned by the John Brown
raid in 1859.

Douglass had known Brown since paying him a visit
in Springfield, Mass., in 1848. Thereafter the relations
between them were cordial. In 1858 Brown spent three
weeks at the Douglass home in Rochester, devoting
much of his time to a Provisional Constitution which he
planned to put into effect after the raid. In August 1858,
two months before he struck, Brown met Douglass at
Chambersburg, Pa., pleading with him to join the
planned raid. Douglass demurred; he would not be
numbered among the five Negroes who took part in the
Harpers Ferry affair. After Brown was captured, however, Douglass sped to Canada, fearful that he might be
seized as an accomplice. Douglass remained abroad for
only five months, brought back in May 1860 by the
death of his fifth and last child, his especially loved
Annie.

If the spring of 1860 was low tide for Douglass, the
autumn brought a Republican president, Abraham Lincoln, a development Douglass had predicted. Having
also said that he had "little hope of the freedom of the
slave by peaceful means," Douglass welcomed the
coming of the Civil War. To him, as to other blacks and
abolitionists in general, the war quickly became a crusade for freedom, nothing more and certainly nothing
less. To this end Douglass called upon the Lincoln administration to recruit Negroes into the Union Army and
to free the slaves as a war measure. The cautious Lincoln, his ear to the ground, ignored such advice, and
scarcely paid more attention to the subsequent sharp
criticism from Douglass and others. But a war, particularly a prolonged war, has realities that could not be
ignored. Hence on Jan. 1, 1863, Lincoln issued the
Emancipation Proclamation, declaring free the slaves in
states still in rebellion and welcoming Negroes into the
Union Armies.

The elated Douglass urged Negroes to enlist and himself became a recruiting agent for two colored Massachusetts regiments, his two oldest sons becoming his
first signees. After one of his two visits to the White
House, Douglass had a conference with Secretary of
War Stanton, from which he got the impression that he
would be granted an assistant adjutantship. He there-
upon announced that he was bringing his journalistic
career to a close. This step was not too painful, his
paper having fallen on lean days. Since 1851 it had
borne his name, *Frederick Douglass' Paper* to 1860,
and *Douglass' Monthly* thereafter. However inglorious

its end, the journalistic career of Douglass was notable
not only for the causes it espoused but as a symbol of
the free press in action, much as its editor's inimitable
public addresses symbolized a tradition of equal importance—freedom of speech. Before abandoning journalism Douglass, as it turned out, might better have waited
until he had an army commission in his hands. Such a
commission never came. Stanton or Lincoln, or both in
concert, having come to the conclusion that a commission to a colored man was at that stage too far in ad-
vance of public opinion.

Douglass turned again to the lecture platform, his
speeches increasingly centering on Negro suffrage. In
1860 he had worked zealously in the vain effort to
repeal the New York constitutional requirement that
Negro men own $250 worth of real estate before they
could vote. In the closing stages of the war, as it became
evident that slavery was on its way out, Douglass and
other Negro leaders gave their major attention to the
suffrage issue. With Douglass in the chair a National
Convention of Colored Men, meeting in Syracuse, N.Y.,
in October 1864, drew up an "Address to the People
of the United States," which asserted that the right to
vote was the keystone of the arch of human liberty.

With the war over, Douglass claimed that the nation
owed a heavy debt to the nearly 200,000 Negroes who
had worn the Union blue. This debt could be paid in
part, he added, by a national policy of equal suffrage for
all. At a White House conference with Andrew Johnson, Lincoln's successor, Douglass and four other colored spokesmen expressed the hope that Negroes
would be fully enfranchised throughout the nation.
When Johnson argued that black voting might lead to a
war of the races, Douglass begged leave to differ, stating
that Negro voting lessened the likelihood of racial conflict. Negroes got little from President Johnson in any
quarter. But in 1870 the Fifteenth Amendment was
ratified, forbidding states to deny the ballot on the
grounds of race, color, or previous servitude. Ratifica-
tion ceremonies were numerous, the largest taking
place in Baltimore in mid-May 1870, with Frederick
Douglass the orator of the day.

Meanwhile, in September 1870 Douglass became
editor of the *New National Era*, a weekly newspaper to
"cheer and strengthen [the recently emancipated
slaves]." He purchased the paper on Dec. 12, 1870,
and published it until September 1874 when he had to
relinquish it due to financial losses incurred when the
Freedmen's Bank failed.

The politically minded Douglass found a natural
home in the Republican party, becoming one of its
staunchest supporters. It was the party of the martyred
Lincoln, and although Douglass was not one of Lincoln's Negro idolaters, he had felt a sense of personal
loss upon his death. Douglass owned Lincoln's walking
cane, sent to him by the widowed Mrs. Lincoln. Moreover, the Republican party's claim to having won the
war had its weight with Douglass. He was, in addition,
always cool to the Democratic party, regarding it not
only in terms of "the bloody shirt," but viewing it as the
political refuge of the Klan types in the rural South and
the black-labor-competitor, working-class whites in the
urban centers of the North.

The fidelity of Douglass was not lost upon the Republican party. In March 1877 President Hayes named him marshal of the District of Columbia, and four years later another Republican administration appointed him recorder of deeds for the District of Columbia. Having moved from Rochester to Washington in 1872, Douglass was not personally inconvenienced by these patronage plums. Indeed these federal appointments had a beneficial effect on Douglass, enabling him to escape the rigors of the lecture circuit.

As an officeholder Douglass took his responsibilities seriously, giving short shrift to job-seekers of questionable competence. While in the marshal's office he stated publicly that his subordinates were "honest, capable, industrious, painstaking and faithful," an assertion that nobody challenged, it seems. Himself putting in a full day's work, he insisted that those under him do likewise. The functions of the marshal's office included surveillance of criminals, and for this aspect of the job Douglass had little enthusiasm. But otherwise he found the appointment to his liking, particularly after the first weeks when he had been under fire by some blacks for not resigning when Hayes removed from the office its ceremonial functions on social occasions held at the White House. But the marshal's office retained its highest honorary function, that of escort at a presidential inauguration, accompanying both the outgoing and incoming chief executives. In performance of this duty, Douglass led the impressive march from the Senate chamber to the Capitol rotunda on March 4, 1881, where James A. Garfield took the oath of office.

The new president appointed Douglass recorder of deeds for the District of Columbia, an exchange of posts which he readily accepted. As in the case of Douglass's previous appointment this was a Negro "first." Douglass held the recordership for five years, since Garfield's successor, President Cleveland, did not call for his resignation immediately. Douglass found the recorder's post easily mastered and somewhat routine, "though specific, exacting, and imperative," as he put it.

During his years in the marshal's and recorder's offices Douglass never felt that he had to hold his tongue on public issues. The charge, made by one critic, that "a fat office gagged him" could hardly hold water. Always outspoken, he continued to hit hard at practices which he considered unwise, unjust, or prejudice-ridden. The most prominent Negro of his day, his words carried weight on both sides of the color line.

On no major issue relating to Negroes during the 1870s and 1880s did Douglass fail to state his views, always leaving no doubt as to where he stood. On many issues his stance was predictable. Obviously he would denounce such developments as the suppression of the Negro vote in the South, the leasing out of convicts as laborers, the crop-lien system, and the prevalence of lynching. He railed against the rulings of the Supreme Court, particularly in voiding the Civil Rights Act of 1875: "Oh, for a Supreme Court in the United States which shall be as true to the claims of humanity as the Supreme Court formerly was to the demands of slavery." Predictably, too, Douglass urged Negroes to support the Cuban insurgents who were struggling to overthrow Spanish rule.

But even on issues which were less clear-cut from a reformist point of view, Douglass did not hesitate to offer his advice. In 1871 he urged Negro Americans to support the Grant administration's efforts to annex Santo Domingo, a position at loggerheads with that of Charles Sumner, the great Senate champion of Negro rights. Later in the decade Douglass vigorously opposed the colored migration to Kansas movement, the "Great Exodus," publicly debating the issue with Richard T. Greener, national secretary of the Emigration Aid Society and the first Negro to be graduated from Harvard College.

During the 1870s and 1880s there was little change in Douglass's long-held economic views of Negro thrift and self-help. Himself moderately well off, his economic orientation was middle class, reflecting something of the acquisitive spirit typical of America's Gilded Age. A believer in self-reliance, Douglass held that the black man's destiny was largely in his own hands, that his white friends could not do for him what he could and should do for himself.

His belief that Negroes should be their own spokesmen did not mean that he favored a policy of "go it alone." In social matters Douglass retained his viewpoint that America was a composite nation and that racial cooperation and amalgamation were the solutions to the color problem. Negroes should become a part of the American community, said Douglass, a component of the "body politic." His belief that a solid and separate Negro minority would tend to polarize black-white relations drew a sharp disapproval from journalist John Edward Bruce: "Mr. Douglass evidently wants to get away from the Negro race, and from the criticism I have heard quite recently of him, he will not meet any armed resistance in his flight."

If a touch of personal pique made Bruce's barb more pointed than the evidence would bear, Douglass himself left no doubt that he did not believe that separation was the way out for the American Negro. His second marriage was an affirmation of this conviction. In January 1884, two years after the death of his first wife, he married Helen Pitts, a white woman of forty-five who had worked in the recorder's office as his secretary. Douglass was fully prepared for the criticism that followed, taking the view that this crowning act of his private life was a concrete demonstration that whites and blacks could live in complete equality under the same roof. Whether Douglass proved anything by his second marriage is conjectural although it certainly could be counted as a congenial union.

In 1886 Douglass, no longer on the federal payroll, took a belated honeymoon. For nearly a year he and Helen traveled throughout Western Europe and the Near East, following the familiar tourist trail in the main. Douglass found the trip stimulating in every way. The famed historic sites inevitably held a deep attraction for an ever-learning, reflective mind such as his. He was also moved by the apparent lack of color prejudice, rejoicing that "I could and did walk the world unquestioned, a man among men."

Shortly after returning home he was approached by

the Republican National Convention to assist the party in the presidential election of 1888. Assigned four key states, he took the stump night and day, despite his seventy years. His reward came when the new chief executive, Benjamin Harrison, appointed him as minister-resident and consul-general to the Republic of Haiti, and chargé d'affaires for the Dominican Republic. Douglass was well received by the Haitians, reflecting their awareness of his long career as a reformer. He proved to be a conscientious official, whether in the performance of routine commercial duties as consul-general or the more ceremonial responsibilities as minister-resident. His first year was relatively calm but in January 1891 he came into the eve of a storm when his government announced its intention to seek a naval lease at Môle St. Nicolas. Douglass favored the lease but, as it turned out, the Haitians did not, politely turning down the offer. Supporters of the project made Douglass the scapegoat, charging that he had been lukewarm in his efforts. Douglass published a lengthy reply but the setback, along with reasons of health, led him to resign in June 1891.

Douglass's five remaining years after his return from Haiti were quiet but far from inactive. He held no federal post and he cut down on his speaking engagements. But he kept busy in writing, corresponding, and accepting the numerous honors that came his way, such as a doctorate of laws from Wilberforce University. Age did not dim his interest in reformist movements. On his last day, Feb. 20, 1895, he had spoken to a meeting of the National Council of Women, held in Washington. That evening he suffered a fatal heart attack. Upon the news of his death one state legislature adjourned for the day out of respect for his memory and four other legislatures adopted resolutions of regret.

He would not be forgotten. Reformers of a later day, particularly Negroes, hailed his name. Sixty years after his death the federal government responded in a number of ways—in purchasing his last home (Anacostia, D.C.) as a national shrine under the National Park Service of the Department of the Interior, in naming a bridge in the nation's capital after him, and in issuing, on Feb. 14, 1967, a twenty-five-cent postage stamp showing his likeness.

Frederick Douglass cast a long shadow because of his sense of humanity and his willingness to battle for his convictions. He is remembered too for his remarkable social insights. No one, for example, pointed out more insistently than he that the status of the Negro was the touchstone of American democracy, its inevitable and ultimate test.

Douglass produced three autobiographies, *Narrative of the Life of Frederick Douglass* (1845), *My Bondage and My Freedom* (1855), three times longer than its predecessor, and *Life and Times of Frederick Douglass* (1881, updated 1892). Of the earlier book-length biographies of Douglass the best is Frederic May Holland's *Frederick Douglass: The Orator* (1891), a clearly written, briskly paced work. In 1948 Benjamin Quarles brought out a full-length volume, *Frederick Douglass*, giving "a balanced account which portrayed him neither as a demi-god or as a demagogue," in the words of Rayford W. Logan in the 1962 Collier Books reprint

of *Life and Times*. In 1964, after bringing out a path-breaking four-volume series, *The Life and Times of Frederick Douglass* (1950–1955), Phillip S. Foner wove together much of the material therein under the title *Frederick Douglass* (1964). A very useful work, this book profited from Foner's professional skills and his extensive research in black and labor history. There is a very brief sketch by William E. B. Du Bois in *DAB* (3:406–7). In 1979 the Yale University Press published the first volume of a projected fourteen-volume edition of *The Frederick Douglass Papers*, edited by John W. Blassingame. — BENJAMIN QUARLES

DOUGLASS, SARAH MAPPS DOUGLASS (1806–1882), teacher and abolitionist. She was born in Philadelphia on Sept. 9, 1806, the daughter of Robert and Grace (Bustill) Douglass. The Bustills were prominent Quakers, her maternal grandfather, Cyril Bustill (1732–1806), having been owner of a bakeshop, a schoolmaster, and an early member of the Free African Society, the first Afro-American benevolent organization. Her mother ran a "Quaker millinery store" next to the family bakery. Her father, perhaps a hairdresser, was one of the founders of the First African Presbyterian Church of Philadelphia.

Privately tutored, she opened a school in Philadelphia for Negro children sometime in the 1820s which the Philadelphia Female Anti-Slavery Society began supporting financially in March 1838. Sarah was then corresponding secretary of the society and attended several abolitionist conventions. Through them she became acquainted with Lucretia Mott, the wife of Robert Purvis, Charlotte Forten (Grimké) and two other daughters of James Forten, a wealthy shipbuilder. More important was the friendship she developed with the white Grimké sisters, Sarah and Angelina, daughters of the Oxford-trained Judge John F. Grimké, a slaveowning justice of the South Carolina Supreme Court. "The girls revolted against the formalism of the Episcopal Church, the shallowness of social life, and the restraints upon education and useful activity for women. They hated the barbarism of slavery and the laws which forbade the education of slaves. Finally, they fled from the stifling environment of the South and went to Philadelphia, where both became Quakers" (Dwight Lowell Dumond, *Anti-Slavery . . . The Crusade for Freedom in America* [1961], pp. 190–91). Not even the Grimké sisters could change the discriminatory practices of the Philadelphia Quakers. They were censured in 1837 for sitting beside Mrs. Douglass and her daughter in the Arch Street Meeting. When Sarah and her mother were among the Negro guests at the wedding of Angelina Grimké and Theodore Weld, a prominent abolitionist, in May 1838, the Philadelphia press condemned it as an intolerable incident of abolitionist "amalgamation practice." Two days later a mob burned down Pennsylvania Hall, the newly built headquarters of the state antislavery society, and set fire to the shelter for colored orphans. This was one of several race riots in Philadelphia: on Aug. 13, 1834, a white mob had wrecked the African Presbyterian church, burned homes, and brutally beaten several Negroes. Similar riots occurred in 1835 and 1842, and in other northern cities during the

Ottley Relates Story of Ex-Slave Who Became Confidant of Lincoln

1st Negro Guest at Inaugural Fete

BY ROI OTTLEY

Awkwardly, a youthful Negro stood up at a public meeting in 1841 and spoke to a group of white people, his first such experience. He was tall and commanding, with deep set eyes, a mass of crisp black hair, and a low, melodious voice.

In full manhood, he became the most distinguished Negro of his day. But that night, he trembled as he groped for words. At length, urged by the sympathy of his listeners, he managed to relate a crude but eloquent story of his experiences as a slave. The audience wept openly. When he finished, one man rose and asked: " Is this a man—or thing? "

The Negro was Frederick Douglass. In 1863 he was introduced to Abraham Lincoln as the spokesman of his race, the beginning of personal contacts with the President that were to touch the wellsprings of the Emancipator's personality and give us profound insights into his feelings toward the Negro at a crucial moment in the country's history.

" I was never more quickly and more completely put at ease in the presence of a great man," said Douglass after his first visit to the White House. " When I entered, he was seated in a low armchair with his feet extended on the floor, surrounded by a large number of documents and several busy secretaries.

Many Talks with Lincoln

" The President appeared to be much overworked and tired. Long lines of care were already deeply written on Mr. Lincoln's brow, and his strong face, full of earnestness, lighted up as soon as my name was mentioned. As I approached he rose and extended his hand, and bade me welcome.

" I at once felt myself in the presence of an honest man— one whom I could love, honor and trust without reserve ⸱ doubt."

Lincoln graciously said, " I know who you are, Mr. Douglass; Mr. Seward has told me all about you. Sit down. I am glad to see you."

Never was Lincoln anything but forthright in his many talks with Douglass, a fact which indicates the respect he had for the Negro. For example, when Douglass once complained that captured Negro soldiers were victims of the South's fury and unwisely urged revenge, the great man's answer was:

" Retaliation is a terrible remedy, and one which is very difficult to apply. If once begun, there is no telling where it will end." And, he bluntly added, Negroes ought to enter the service under any condition, because of their vast stake in the conflict.

Invited to Reception

But a few months after the promulgation of the Emancipation Proclamation, he had the great humility to admit to the Negro that he might have failed in his intention. " The slaves," he said, " are not coming so rapidly and so numerously to us as I had hoped." He asked Douglass' counsel. The Negro sought to allay his fears by saying it was very probable that, in some sections, slaves had not heard of the proclamation.

When Lincoln was reelected, and invited a Negro to the inauguration reception for the first time in history, he might have been serving notice that Negroes should be treated as social equals. Whatever the reason, Frederick Douglass so interpreted the invitation. But two disagreeable policemen did not share the President's liberalism, and refused to admit the Negro, who was accompanied by a lady.

Luckily, a gentleman was passing who recognized the Negro leader. " Be so kind," Douglass asked, " as to say to Mr. Lincoln that Frederick Douglass is detained by officers at the door." He afterward remarked, " 'The policemen were simply complying with an old custom, the outgrowth of slavery, as dogs will sometimes rub their necks, long after their collars are removed, thinking they are still there.' "

Opinion Respected

Before long, Douglass walked into the East Room of the Executive Mansion, amid such elegance as the ex-slave had never seen. He was the cynosure of every eye. As he approached, the President happily exclaimed, "Here comes my friend Douglass!"

He took the Negro by the arm and led him aside. "I am glad to see you. I saw you in the crowd today, listening to my address. How did you like it? " Douglass declined to detain him. " No, no," Lincoln insisted, "you must stop a little, Douglass. There is no man in the country whose opinions I value more than yours."

Douglass afterwards said: "I felt myself a man among men! "

The day Lincoln's assassination was announced, so legend says, no Negro spoke above a whisper. But within a month, thousands of donations poured into a Negro committee, which had been formed to plan the erection of a monument. Eleven years later the first memorial to the great man was unveiled in Lincoln Park, Washington, D. C., paid for entirely by Negroes. And Frederick Douglass made the speech of tribute.

FREDERICK DOUGLASS PICKS ROCHESTER AS HEADQUARTERS FOR HIS FIGHT AGAINST SLAVERY

By DR. BLAKE McKELVEY
Historian, City of Rochester

FREDERICK AUGUSTUS WASHINGTON BAILEY, who took the name of Douglass after his escape from slavery, made his home in Rochester from 1847 until 1872. Already widely noted for his *Autobiography* first published in 1845, he soon won the respect of many in the area and attracted local support for his newspaper and other ventures. He became an effective leader of the small group of Negro residents and with the aid of numerous white friends championed their cause in local, state, and national affairs. As his stature grew, he emerged as the leader of his race, and as the outstanding Rochesterian of his day; he is today honored as one of the city's three or four most distinguished citizens.

Born a slave in Maryland in 1817, Frederick Douglass fled to New Bedford, Massachusetts, in 1838 and soon became an active agent of that State's anti-slavery society. His dramatic personal experiences, his strikingly handsome appearance, and his talents as a public speaker quickly won many friends there and in England, which he visted in 1845 and where generous sympathizers purchased his freedom and subscribed a fund to support his further work in the States. Back in America, he made an extended speaking tour throughout the North with William Garrison in 1847 and chose Rochester as the site for his contemplated

Though public funds were tight in 1897, New York State legislature readily appropriated $3,000, one third total cost, for 17-foot-high Douglass monument in Rochester.
Photo courtesy of Rochester Public Library

19

paper, THE NORTH STAR, an anti-slavery weekly to be printed and published by Negroes.

Well acquainted with anti-slavery leaders throughout the country, Douglass brought an array of outside resources to back his venture in Rochester. He engaged Martin R. Delany, formerly editor of a Negro paper in Pittsburgh, and William C. Nell, a Negro follower of Garrison, as his associates and set up his press in the basement of the African Methodist Episcopal Zion Church. An English friend, Miss Julia Griffiths, soon joined his staff and became its mainstay and chief editorial consultant for many years.

Douglass purchased a comfortable house on Alexander Street on the eastern side of the city in a setting which proved more congenial for his many visitors than for his wife and children who found few associates close by. He himself quickly developed many friends throughout the city — the Anthonys, the Posts, the Moores, the Porters, old William C. Bloss, and many others. He enjoyed a cordial welcome in their homes and among the Quaker and Unitarian congregations as well as in the Zion Church where he spoke frequently. But his extended speaking tours and other journeys often kept him on the road for months at a time and checked any close identity with local affairs except those directly related to his major concern.

One exception involved the issue of school discrimination. The establishment of a special school for Negro children in 1841 had antedated his arrival. Determined to save his oldest daughter, Rosetta, from the indignities of a segregated school, he enrolled her in the private school conducted by Miss Tracy on Alexander Street. When he learned that even this sympathetic lady was instructing his daughter in private in order not to affront the parents of some other pupils, he indignantly sent her to a private school in Albany, and later to Oberlin College. Few Negroes could make such provisions or undertake to employ a private tutor as Douglass did (Miss Phebe Thayer, a Quaker) for the younger children. Douglass joined with Everard Peck and William Bloss in a campaign in 1849 to persuade the city to abandon its Negro school and to open all public schools to their unrestricted attendance. While defeated at the time, they did secure the opening of School No. 13 on the east side as an integrated school for Negro and white children in the southeast district. Some of the younger Douglasses attended there for a time, and in 1857 Rochester finally recognized the stupidity of segregation and admitted all Negro children to the regular city schools.

In this and other activities Douglass made an impact on the city and its Negro residents. His eloquent oratory attracted crowds not only to the Zion Church but also on several occasions to Corinthian Hall, the largest auditorium in the city, and he conducted a course of lectures there one winter. He engaged that hall for the public sessions of the National Negro Convention which met at Rochester in July, 1853. This important gathering attracted 140 Negro delegates from other cities and

20

revived a movement for Negro unity which had lapsed for several years. Douglass, who had presided at the previous convention, now served as chairman of the resolutions committee and brought in a memorable "Declaration of Sentiments."

It proclaimed broad objectives for Negroes. As free Americans, they declared that "the doors of the school-house, the workshop, the church, the college, shall be thrown open as freely to our children as to the children of other members of the community," that "the white and black may stand on an equal footing before the laws of the land," that "the complete and unrestricted right of suffrage, which is essential to the dignity even of the white man, be extended to the Free Colored Man also." The convention not only endorsed these resolutions but approved another measure introduced by Douglass for the establishment of a manual training school for Negroes. The latter proposal had been debated for many years and an abortive attempt to achieve it had occurred at New Haven, Connecticut. The renewed effort to establish such a school at Rochester or at Erie, Pennsylvania, likewise failed, but the Rochester meeting aired most of the issues that would trouble Negro-white relations for many decades to come.

One issue that needed clarification was the basic question of political action. Douglass had broken with Garrison several years before, partly because of this tactical issue. He had found many of his Rochester friends agreed on the possibility and desirability of abolishing slavery under the constitution by political means, and he had become increasingly identified with local Liberty party forces and was their candidate for the Assembly in 1851 and for Secretary of State at Albany in 1855. The next year he endorsed, after much hesitation, the newly formed Republican party as the most practical alternative to the Southern-dominated Democratic party.

While politics divided some of the anti-slavery workers, other concerns drew them together. Douglass found many of his white and colored friends ready to help in the dangerous task of aiding fugitive slaves escape to Canada. Rochester's proximity to the border, near the mouth of a long north-flowing river, made it a depot on the Underground Railroad, and the wide fame of Frederick Douglass made his home and his printing shop the first destination of many fugitives. He became the chief local agent and directed the efforts of a dozen Rochester confederates who assisted some 400 freedom-loving Negroes to escape to Canada. He worked closely with Harriet Tubman who "carried the war into Africa" and became, in Douglass's phrase, the "Moses of her people." And he valued the assistance of the Isaac Posts, the Daniel Anthonys, and other Rochester followers of Garrison as well as that of William C. Bloss, Samuel D. Porter, Gideon Pitts, and their political allies.

Their new sense of kinship was strengthened by the frequent visits in Rochester of John Brown, another old friend of Douglass. Brown's zeal not only kindled local ardor for the struggle to save Kansas, but also enlisted one Rochester follower, Shields Green, for his more desperate raid on Harpers Ferry. Douglass, who was strongly drawn to this forthright champion of Negro rights, was long a close consultant on his plans, but he drew back in 1859 from the direct attack on a federal arsenal. When Brown nevertheless pressed forward and met disaster, Douglass had to flee the country, leaving his family and associates in Rochester to carry on his papers the best they could.

Although Douglass had achieved a remarkable career, his newspaper was but a minor factor in that success. Discouraged by the response of his fellow Negroes to a journal of their own, Douglass had joined forces with Gerrit Smith and merged the latter's LIBERTY PARTY PAPER with his NORTH STAR to make FREDERICK DOUGLASS' PAPER, as it was called after June, 1851. He added a monthly seven years later but seldom managed to meet publishing expenses without frequent subventions from Smith or from his own British backers. Douglass discontinued the weekly in July, 1860, shortly after his return to Rochester.

The distraught editor had come back to comfort his family after the death of his youngest daughter, Annie, "the light and life of my house." He found the Presidential campaign already started and took a keen interest in its development. Despite a preference for Seward, Douglass endorsed Lincoln after his nomination by the Republicans and urged his support by Negroes and abolitionists. But in August he attended a hastily called convention of radical abolitionists at Syracuse and impulsively joined in the nomination of Gerrit Smith. He soon, however,

Frederick Douglass died in Washington, D. C., in 1895, was buried in Rochester. Indicative of Rochester's esteem for Negro leader, a crowd of 10,000 attended 1898 unveiling of his monument in downtown business district. Lofty memorial was later moved to a suburban park.

lost enthusiasm for a protest vote and worked actively for Lincoln's election during the last weeks. Yet his major concern was to secure a repeal of the New York law limiting Negro voters to those who owned property valued at $250. His failure in this effort cast a gloom over the election returns.

Douglass became so despondent after his defeat on the suffrage issue that he began for the first time to support the emigration movement. He had long opposed that strategy and had encouraged local Negroes to oppose it. The continued flight of refugees to Canada had carried off many, even of his fellows in Rochester, where their numbers had remained fairly stationary since the mid-thirties while the city's population had quadrupled. Douglass now gave a sympathetic word of encouragement to a band of 12 local Negro families whose 52 members set out, in March, 1861, under the leadership of a Baptist Negro clergyman to find new homes in Haiti. He endorsed the efforts of his old partner, Delany, to recruit emigrants for Liberia and aided his son, Lewis, in plans to establish a Negro colony in Central America.

Yet Lincoln's determined stand against the secessionist states stirred his spirits. He hopefully viewed the war as a battle to free the slaves and urged official recognition of that objective. Though often discouraged by what appeared to be a vacillating policy on Lincoln's part, Douglass hailed the provisional Emancipation Proclamation, of September, 1862, as a decisive victory and rejoiced when emancipation was proclaimed effective on January 1, 1863. He threw himself into the work of obtaining Negro recruits for military service, and journeyed to Washington in July, 1863, to meet Lincoln; he urged the President to grant full pay and other equal treatment for Negro soldiers. Although denied that assurance he gladly accepted the promise of an appointment to recruit Negroes in the South. He hastily terminated the publication of his monthly in August, to take up that hazardous task, but when the commission failed to arrive, he continued his lecture program instead.

Douglass had moved his family from Alexander Street to a more spacious site on South Avenue just beyond the city's border in 1852. The new location had been admirable as a haven for refugees, and although that function was now terminated, the house provided a comfortable home. But Douglass had little opportunity to enjoy its rural charms since a busy schedule of lectures kept him on the road. He was frequently mentioned for various official posts. The Democratic UNION AND ADVERTISER badgered local Republicans to name him for Congress in 1868 and again in 1870. President Grant did appoint him as secretary of a commission to San Domingo in 1871 and local Republicans nominated him for the Assembly that year. He ran barely 1200 votes behind his successful opponent on that occasion, despite his absence from the district throughout the contest. The destruction of his home by fire in 1872 aroused suspicions of incendiarism and finally broke his ties with Rochester; he moved his family to Washington shortly thereafter.

THE MILITARY LINCOLN

THE subject of Abraham Lincoln in the role of Commander - in - Chief brought together two noted Americans, General Dwight D. Eisenhower and Bruce Catton, Pultizer Prize historian, in an NBC-TV tribute to the Civil War President on the eve of Lincoln's birthday. The coast-to-coast program was titled, "Eisenhower on Lincoln—a Military Memoir."

The setting for the video-taped program was Gettysburg—the hallowed ground of the battlefield itself, as well as the library in the Eisenhower farm home, nearby. The former President's intense interest in Gettysburg dates back to 1918 when as a young Army captain he was stationed there for a year in command of World War I troops. In spare moments he explored the Gettysburg Battlefield in "a little old car" and time and again returned to the spot where Lincoln delivered his brief but immortal Gettysburg Address.

The grasp and knowledge of the five-star general as a student of Lincoln's military leadership has won the respect of historians. In his informal discussion with Mr. Catton, he stated his views on Lincoln's problem-laden relations with his Union generals, and read the caustic letter Lincoln wrote to General Meade but never sent. General Eisenhower touched upon Jefferson Davis as the Rebel leader, and Robert E. Lee as the brilliant Confederate general. In one of the program's lighter moments, he spoke briefly of himself as an amateur artist, admitting his failure to master the knack of getting Lee's white beard down on canvas.

But it was Lincoln, with his two-fold burden of directing the war and guiding the affairs of state, upon whom General Eisenhower concentrated. He explained his belief that Lincoln's words and actions of a century ago have more meaning for Americans today than then.

★   ★   ★   ★   ★

Prior to the telecast, Mr. Catton, in his capacity as Chairman, NYCWCC, and Carl Haverlin, Secretary, visited Albany that same day (February 11) to participate with Governor Nelson A. Rockefeller and other State leaders in launching the year-long State-wide observance of the centennial of Abraham Lincoln's Emancipation Proclamation.

CATTON HAILS WROW
ON HERITAGE SERIES

BRUCE CATTON, NYCWCC Chairman, praises highly a daily radio series inaugurated recently by Station WROW, Albany, carrying to listeners over a wide area of the Northeast the story of New York State's role in the Civil War. The noted historian terms it "a prime example of broadcasters at work in the public cause."

Drawing largely on historical material in the NYCWCC monthly publication NEW YORK

BOB WALLACE

STATE AND THE CIVIL WAR, the WROW staff has composed more than 40 dramatic narratives, each of about three minutes duration, that are heard periodically throughout the broadcasting day. This "heritage of history" series is narrated by veteran WROW newsman Bob Wallace. Tape-recorded, it will become part of the audio collection of Civil War material to be preserved by the Catton Commission.

New York State lends Lincoln's original Emancipation Proclamation to American History Workshop at Rutgers University. Holding the document's four pages are: Everett Landers, New Jersey CWCC; Donald Sinclair, special collections curator at Rutgers; Donald F. Cameron, Rutgers librarian; N. J. State Trooper Stanley Hetman, and Floyd Hardy, of the N. Y. S. Library
Picture by Rutgers News Service

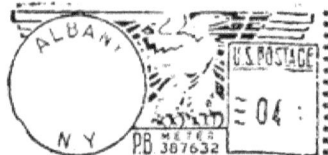

Mr. R. Gerald McCarthy
Lincoln Natural Life Foundation
Fort Wayne, Ind.

THINGS TO NOTE
ON TITLE PAGE:

SENATOR BARRETT

Senator Elisha T. Barrett, Brightwaters, L. I., sponsor of legislation creating NYCWCC and a MEMBER (Executive Committee) became an *ex-officio member* when named by Senate Majority Leader Walter Mahoney to Chairman of the Senate Finance Committee, replacing Senator Austin W. Erwin, Geneseo, who did not seek re-election to the Senate.

Assemblyman Felipe N. Torres, New York City, not seeking re-election, relinquished his Commission membership to Assemblyman Lloyd E. Dickens, also of N.Y.C., by appointment of Assembly Speaker Joseph F. Carlino.

The Commission thanks Mr. Torres for his valued contributions as a charter member, and welcomes his successor.

The Columbia Historical Society

Newsletter

1307 New Hampshire Avenue, N. 1
Washington, D. C. 20036
November 26, 1969

> NEXT REGULAR MEETING
> Christian Heurich Mansion
> 1307 New Hampshire Avenue, N.W.
> Wednesday, December 10, 1969
> 8 P.M

Dear Member

At the meeting on the 10th of December we shall hear from a distinguished architect about the "Proposed Extension of the West Central Front of the United States Capitol." The Speaker, Mr. Mario E. Capioli, Assistant Architect of the Capitol, is well-known. He was born in Italy, one of the great art centers of the world, and came to the United States in 1911. After engaging in the private practice of architecture in New York City for twenty years he served as Director of Architecture of Colonial Williamsburg, 1949 1957. During the next two years he was in private practice here in Washington. He has been Assistant Architect of the Capitol for the last ten years.

With the enactment of Public Law 91-109 earlier this month, the restoration of "Cedar Hill" at 1411 W Street, S. E. has been made possible. It will enable the National Park Service to convert the Frederick Douglass Home into a fitting memorial to that one-time Maryland slave who became such a dynamic leader in the abolitionist movement and was one of President Lincoln's advisors. Cedar Hill is now destined to become a significant visitors site in our National Capitol. I am grateful to our Recorder, Mr. William Ellis, for presenting my endorsement on behalf of the Society at last month's hearing of Senator Hart's bill during the long legislative journey of the Public Law.

As some early editions of the Society's "Records" indicate, our interest in Frederick Douglass as an internationally known resident of Washington is nothing new. They also show that Cedar Hill's previous owner, John VanHook, was commended by President Lincoln and General Grant for important missions he carried out during that critical period in our Nation's history. An article about Cedar Hill and its interesting owners is being prepared for the next volume of our Records by Mr. O. Kenneth Baker of the Society. He would appreciate any pertinent items of information that other members might be able to contribute.

THE DOUGLASS MURAL

It was former director Adam Strohm who said, "Mean surroundings make mean people; things of beauty cleanse our hearts." This philosophy is reflected in the fact that the Detroit Public Library's branch agencies are attractive, comfortable buildings, rather than merely utilitarian; and it caused the Main Library to be designed, in architecture and decoration, so as to become one of the most handsome public buildings in the country.

The newest piece of decorative art work to be added was dedicated Sunday, May 14, 1972. Leroy Foster's mural, "The Life and Times of Frederick Douglass," was installed over the charge desk of the Frederick Douglass Branch Library in Scripps Park. This handsome mural painting depicts incidents in the life of the noted abolitionist and orator, a one-time slave who risked his safety and freedom to become an advocate of his people, and who was an influential official in the government of President Lincoln.

The mural highlights a significant moment in Detroit history: March 12, 1859, when Frederick Douglass met with John Brown and seven prominent black Detroiters—William Lambert, George De-Baptiste, Joseph Ferguson, William Webb, Rev. William C. Monroe, Willie Wilson, and John Jackson—to discuss their common goals and aims. A marker on William Webb's house on East Congress between St. Antoine and Hastings has hitherto been the only memorial to that meeting.

The Foster mural was commissioned by the International Afro-American Museum, 1553 West Grand Boulevard, near the Lothrop Branch Library. A fortunate series of circumstances made this gift possible: the decision of the Detroit Library Commission to name the newest branch library after Douglass; the interest of the I.A.M. in having a historical mural about Douglass created; the ambition of artist Leroy Foster to create such a mural; and the agreement of all the parties to honor the namesake branch library as the home of the mural. The Library was able to obtain a grant matching the funds raised by the Museum, both being applied to the cost of the mural.

A color reproduction of the mural is being prepared for publication in post card form.　　　　　　　　　　　　　　　　　　　　　—JCD

Editor's Note

This is the season to color the Library's Publications Office staff red, white, and blue and sprinkle it with stars. This office, which is responsible for the *Quarterly Journal*, is surrounded by manuscripts for the forthcoming American Revolution Bicentennial publications as well as for folders, flyers, programs, and kits for events offered in the Library's Bicentennial program.

A collection of pamphlets published under the title *English Defenders of American Freedoms, 1774–1778*, was delivered from the printer shortly before this issue goes to press. The five authors of the six pamphlets, which were all written in defense of America after the North Ministry turned to coercion, are Jonathan Shipley, Bishop of St. Asaph; Matthew Robinson-Morris, Baron Rokeby; Catharine Macaulay; John Cartwright; and Willoughby Bertie, Earl of Abingdon. Paul Smith of the Library's American Revolution Bicentennial Office wrote the general introduction plus introductions to each pamphlet. The book, priced at $2.75, is available from the Superintendent of Documents.

Papers delivered at the Library's first symposium on the American Revolution, held May 5 and 6, will be published during the coming fiscal year. Centering on the theme, "The Development of a Revolutionary Mentality," the symposium attracted historians from foreign countries as well as the United States. Speakers at the two-day program were Richard B. Morris, who presided over the sessions, Henry S. Commager, Caroline Robbins, Richard L. Bushman, Pauline Maier, and Mary Beth Norton. Commentators, whose remarks will also be published, were J. H. Plumb, Edmund S. Morgan, Jack P. Greene, and Esmond Wright.

Other Bicentennial publications, which exist now only in hundreds of typewritten manuscript pages, include a checklist of prints in the Library of Congress that relate to the American Revolution, a guide to manuscript sources at LC for the study of the American Revolution, and a reading list for young people. These publications will be announced in the professional and scholarly press as they appear.   SLW

Frederick

Douglass

Black
Imperishable

by Benjamin Quarles

On January 17, 1972, the papers of Frederick Douglass, famed abolitionist, orator, and journalist, were transferred from the National Park Service to the Library of Congress. For many years the Douglass papers had remained at "Cedar Hill," Frederick Douglass' home in the Anacostia section of Washington, D.C., passing from the Frederick Douglass family into the care of the Frederick Douglass Memorial and Historical Association. In 1964 the papers were acquired along with the home by the National Park Service.

Included in the collection are more than 5,000 items, predominantly letters received by Douglass. Manuscripts of Douglass' addresses, speeches, lectures, and articles are amply represented. Most of the collection relates to the career of Douglass during and following the Civil War, the period in which the mass of

American Negroes looked to him for leadership. It is believed that his ante bellum papers were destroyed when the Douglass home in Rochester, N.Y., burned.

The presentation ceremony in the Whittall Pavilion at the Library of Congress was attended by members of the Douglass family, representatives of the Frederick Douglass Memorial and Historical Association, and scholars and officials from the Washington, D.C., area. Benjamin Quarles, Professor of History at Morgan State College in Baltimore and Honorary Consultant in American History to the Library of Congress, delivered the address presented here. Dr. Quarles wrote the biography Frederick Douglass and is also author of The Negro in the American Revolution, Lincoln and the Negro, The Negro in the Making of America, and Black Abolitionists.

To take part in these exercises this morning is an honor which I deeply appreciate. I have always found it stimulating to turn my attention to Frederick Douglass, and it is especially gratifying to speak of him in this particular city in which he spent a quarter of a century. It is likewise a pleasure to speak of Douglass at an observance under the distinguished auspices of the United States Library of Congress.

This is not the first time that Frederick Douglass has been honored by an agency of the Federal Government. Ten years ago his Anacostia Heights home was purchased as a national shrine under the National Parks Service of the Department of the Interior. Since that year, the Federal Government has named a bridge in this city after Douglass, and on February 14, 1967, the Post Office issued a 25-cent stamp of general issue in commemoration of the 150th anniversary of his birth.

These honors to Douglass in recent years and this mark of esteem to him today at this national repository of learning seem highly appropriate. A man of no mean stature, Frederick Douglass cast a long shadow because of his sense of humanity and his willingness to battle for his convictions. He is remembered for his remarkable social insights. No one, for example, pointed out more insistently than he that the Negro was the touchstone of American democracy, its inevitable and ultimate test.

In reviewing the career of this public-spirited American, the usable past comes into its own. His words have a contemporary ring, and his viewpoint and outlook are scarcely less instructive for our day than for his. If today the minority rights struggle has become a major concern in our country, certainly this warrants a fresh look at the race relations reformers of the 19th century. If today the voice of the black American is being listened to as never before, certainly this justifies a fresh hearing of an eloquent black reformer who lived in a day

as unquiet as our own. If today, on the eve of America's Bicentennial, we are examining anew the validity of the principles which our country proclaimed at its birth, we would do well to summon to mind a figure like Frederick Douglass to whom the Declaration of Independence was a lodestar.

Douglass was a figure of heroic proportions. "Were ever so many miracles crowded into a single life?" asked a contemporary. The day and year of his birth are uncertain, for he was born a slave. But when he died five State legislatures adopted resolutions of regret, and at his last rites, held in Washington on a winter afternoon in 1895, two United States Senators and a Supreme Court Justice were numbered among the honorary pallbearers. A *Washington Post* editorial stated that he "died in an epoch which he did more than any other to create."

Douglass, indeed, did symbolize many characteristic American traits, perhaps most obviously the driving force to pull oneself up by the bootstraps. After 20 years in slavery, he fled to New Bedford, Mass., where for three years he lived a hand-to-mouth existence. Things took a turn for the better in 1841 when he became an abolitionist lecturer, following the accidental discovery of a fluent tongue and a talent for the public platform.

His subsequent career reflected the central issues of his times. In 1847 at Rochester, N.Y., he became editor of an antislavery weekly which he published for 16 years. In 1848 he took a prominent part in the Seneca Falls Convention in New York, which formally inaugurated the women's rights movement in this country. A confidant of John Brown, he fled the United States within three days after the unsuccessful raid at Harpers Ferry. During the Civil War he recruited troops for the Union Army, and he urged the Lincoln administration to strike forcefully against slavery. After the war he worked for a Reconstruction policy that would guarantee the right to vote without respect to race.

Beginning in 1877 he received high Federal appointments from successive Republican administrations, becoming in turn Marshal of the District of Columbia, Recorder of Deeds for the District, and Minister to the Republic of Haiti.

Frederick Douglass has a twofold importance. He was both a social critic and an activist. As a critic he directed his fire at any policy or practice which to him was contrary to the great principles which were proclaimed at the birth of the American Republic. More than an armchair observer, Douglass fashioned his life as "a terror to evil-doers," to use the phrase he used to describe his first published journal, *The North Star*. Possessed of a lucid and penetrating intelligence and a sense of determination, Douglass was doubly effective in his attack upon the social ills of his day.

In acquiring the papers of the public-spirited Frederick Douglass, the Library of Congress adds notably to its already incomparable manuscript holdings. Douglass' own writings are models of clarity and good literary form. He never wrote an article or gave a speech without careful preparation. An examination of his manuscripts in this collection being transmitted today will show that Douglass would often write a passage over and over again, striving for the precise word, for the telling phrase. To follow a Douglass line of thought is no chore, although in reading his formal addresses we must be prepared for the long sentences and paragraphs so typical of 19th-century literary expression. Incapable of writing a dull line, Douglass invests his sentences with an almost poetic cadence, compelling the reader to turn the page.

In addition to the writings of the man himself, the Douglass papers that now come to the Library of Congress are wide ranging in both content and texture. They embrace petitions, legal documents, original poems, invitations, newspaper clippings, and, perhaps the most important of all, letters to Douglass.

Those who wrote to Douglass came from various walks of life. They included whites who castigated him as well as those who saw eye to eye with him. Letters came to Douglass from other blacks, some of them prominent like himself but by no means all. These letters by blacks are especially revealing. In them we see black men and women setting their own priorities, articulating their own aspirations. These letters demonstrate anew the ongoing effort of black Americans to take a hand in their own destiny, playing as large a role as humanly possible.

Proud of being black, Douglass also prided himself on being an American. Just as he made it a point to speak to all America, so this collection of papers holds an interest for all Americans. Hence it is not inappropriate that these Douglass papers should repose in the Library of Congress. A national archive, its holdings would as a matter of course be as multiethnic as the American people, as pluralistic as American culture. This transfer of the Douglass papers to the Library of Congress is significant not only for the intrinsic importance of the materials themselves but also as a symbol of the Library's inclusiveness, of its awareness that as Americans on the threshold of our Bicentennial celebration, we must view our country, past and present, in a newer and wider perspective.

Afro-American elements are deeply imbedded in our national character and experience. It is fitting, then, that black documents and source materials should find lodgment in our national library in our Nation's Capital.

Owen Wister
Champion of Old Charleston

by Julian Mason

November, 1975   Bulletin of The Lincoln National Life Foundation . Mark E. Neely, Jr., Editor. Published each month   Number 1653
by The Lincoln National Life Insurance Company, Fort Wayne, Indiana 46801

Emancipation: 113 Years Later

Editor's Note: I am indebted to Professor G. S. Boritt, formerly of Washington University in Saint Louis, for bringing the paper on which this *Lincoln Lore* is based to my attention. I am especially indebted to his student, Yvette Fulcher, for allowing me to see the results of her industrious survey of opinion on Abraham Lincoln among blacks today and to use that study as the basis for this article. I am performing strictly a reporter's role here. Ms. Fulcher asked all the questions, tabulated all the answers, and, in a word, did all the work. She had excellent guidance. Professor Boritt is the author of numerous articles on Lincoln, including "A Case of Political Suicide? Lincoln and the Mexican War" in the *Journal of the Illinois State Historical Society*, and the forthcoming "The Voyage to the Colony of Linconia: The Sixteenth President, Black Colonization, and the Defense Mechanism of Avoidance." He is working on a book on Lincoln's economic thought. Ms. Fulcher was a freshman student in Professor Boritt's course on Abraham Lincoln last year and has, I am sure all will agree, a most promising future ahead of her.

It should be remembered that Ms. Fulcher attempts to quantify the unquantifiable. She had to make allowances in her final tabulations for intensity of feeling, tone of response, etc. Incidentally, the introductory remarks are altogether mine and are based, in part, on James M. McPherson's useful collection, *The Negro's Civil War: How American Negroes Felt and Acted during the War for the Union* (New York, 1965).

M. E. N., Jr.

Skepticism among some black people greeted even Abraham Lincoln's first appearance on the national scene in 1860. H. Ford Douglass, an Illinois black leader, suggested at an abolitionist picnic on the Fourth of July in Framingham, Massachusetts, that "Abraham Lincoln is simply a Henry Clay Whig, and he believes just as Henry Clay believed . . . And Henry Clay was just as odious to the anti-slavery cause and anti-slavery men as ever was John C. Calhoun . . . ." By degrees, the black orator worked up to the drastic assertion that "Abraham Lincoln . . . is on the side of this Slave Power . . . , that has possession of the Federal Government." Douglass was misinformed on at least one point, for he said that Lincoln's proposal was "to let the people and the Territories regulate their domestic institutions in their own way." This was the solution, of course, of Stephen Douglas but not of Abraham Lincoln.

From the Lincoln National Life Foundation
FIGURE 1. Professor Benjamin Quarles

H. Ford Douglass represented only a minority among the black minority in 1860, and by 1865, his opinions had surely shrunk in influence. Even the first cautious rumblings of Lincoln's great emancipation policy were enthusiastically greeted by black men. When a message to Congress of March 6, 1862, suggested federal compensation to any state which moved to abolish slavery gradually, the *Anglo-African*, a Negro newspaper, called it "an event which sent a thrill of joy throughout christendom." The paper called it "a stroke of policy, grandly reticent on the part of its author, yet most timely and sagacious, which has secured for Abraham Lincoln a confidence and admiration on the part of the people, the whole loyal people, such as no man has enjoyed in the present era." Lincoln's Emancipation Proclamation increased the enthusiasm in a crescendo which erupted into wild rejoicing when, on April 4, 1865, the Great Emancipator visited the conquered capital of the Confederacy. A Negro correspondent reported the scene of Lincoln's visit to Richmond this way:

The great event after the capture of the city was the arrival of President Lincoln in it . . . There is no describing the scene along the route. The colored population was wild with enthusiasm. Old men thanked God in a very boisterous manner, and old women shouted upon the pavement as high as they had ever done at a religious revival. . . .

Everyone declares that Richmond never before presented such a spectacle of jubilee. It must be confessed that those who participated in the informal reception of the President were mainly negroes. There were many whites, but they were lost in the great concourse of American citizens of African descent. . . .

I visited yesterday several of the slave jails, where men, women, and children were confined, or herded, for the examination of purchases . . . The owners, as soon as they were aware that we were coming, opened wide the doors and told the confined inmates they

were free. The poor souls could not realize it until they saw the Union army. Even then they thought it must be a pleasant dream, but when they saw Abraham Lincoln they were satisfied that their freedom was perpetual. One enthusiastic old negro woman exclaimed: "I know that I am free, for I have seen Father Abraham and felt him."

When the President returned to the flag-ship of Admiral Porter, in the evening, he was taken from the wharf in a cutter. Just as he pushed off, amid the cheering of the crowd, another good old colored female shouted, "Don't drown Massa Abe, for God's sake!"

After President Lincoln was assassinated ten days later, Edgar Dinsmore, a black soldier from New York, wrote his fiancee:

We mourn for the loss of our great and good President as a loss irreparable. Humanity has lost a firm advocate, our race its Patron Saint, and the good of all the world a fitting object to emulate. . . . The name Abraham Lincoln will ever be cherished in our hearts, and none will more delight to lisp his name in reverence than the future generations of our people.

Most Lincoln students have suspected for some time that the predictions of eternal reverence for Lincoln on the part of American Negroes have proved to be in error. There have been some undercurrents of ambivalence all along. At the inaugural ceremonies of the Freedmen's Memorial Monument to Abraham Lincoln in Washington, D. C., on April 14, 1876, "nearly all of the colored organizations in the city" heard Frederick Douglass, black abolitionist, give a memorable and prophetic address. He pointed out carefully that this was the first occasion on which black Americans "have sought to do honor to any American great man." Before Abraham Lincoln, he intimated, Negroes had had no reason to celebrate American history. Then, warning his audience that "Truth is proper and beautiful at all times and in all places," Douglass dropped his bombshell: "Abraham Lincoln was not, in the fullest sense of the word, either our man or our model . . . He was pre-eminently the white man's President. . . ." Douglass conceded to his "white fellow-citizens, a pre-eminence in this worship" of Lincoln. "You are the children of Abraham Lincoln," he said. "We are at best only his step-children, children by adoption, children by force of circumstances and necessity." Douglass then catalogued the inadequacies he found in Lincoln's policies. Above all, "He was ready and willing at any time during the first years of his administration to deny, postpone and sacrifice the rights of humanity in the colored people, to promote the welfare of the white people of this country. . . . the Union was more to him than our freedom or our future. . . ." The specific charges were these:

. . . he tarried long in the mountain; . . . he strangely told us that we were the cause of the war; . . . he still more strangely told us to leave the land in which we were born; . . . he refused to employ our arms in the defence of the Union; . . . after accepting our services as colored soldiers, he refused to retaliate when we were murdered as colored prisoners; . . . he told us he would save the Union if he could with slavery; . . . he revoked the proclamation of emancipation of General Fremont; . . . he refused to remove the commander of the Army of the Potomac, who was more zealous in his efforts to protect slavery than suppress rebellion. . . .

Except for quotable quotes illustrating Lincoln's racial views before the Civil War, Douglass had laid out the black case against Lincoln largely as it has been laid out ever since by any black who disliked him. The quotable quotes and the public controversy necessary to make the case against Lincoln a subject for popular consumption were both provided, ironically, by the Citizens' Councils of America, white Southern groups which opposed passage of the 1964 Civil Rights Act. In advertisements widely printed in major American newspapers, including the Washington Post, in February of 1964, the Citizens' Councils claimed that three quotations represented "Lincoln's Hopes for the Negro In His Own Words." Two of the three dealt with colonization, and the third was an answer to Stephen Douglas, protesting that he (Lincoln) was not "in favor of bringing about in any way the social and poli-

tical equality of the white and black races." The irony of this campaign was that it may have convinced blacks and left whites unconvinced. Congressman Fred Schwengel of Iowa, a member of the Bibliography Committee for Lincoln Lore, commented simply: "Sedulous selection, it is well known, can make the Scriptures seem the work of Satan."

Nevertheless, a period of black disillusionment, epitomized by Lerone F. Bennett's article in Ebony in 1968 ("Was Abe Lincoln a White Supremacist?"), began, and it has apparently reached deeply into the black community.

We can be sure of very little in this area because, despite its being a topic on which almost everyone has an opinion, scientific surveys of Negro opinion on Abraham Lincoln are few and far between. A brief check of our files at the Lincoln National Life Foundation uncovered no such surveys whatever. Therefore, the significance of Yvette Fulcher's survey of "The Attitudes of Blacks Today Toward Abraham Lincoln" is great. It provides us with our first concrete sampling of this very important segment of opinion on Abraham Lincoln.

Ms. Fulcher's survey was conducted by mail. One hundred twenty persons were contacted and all but thirteen responded. The questions were designed so as not to be loaded in favor of one answer or another and so as to be understandable to "not only a black Representative in the United States Congress . . . , but also a black former convict with an eighth grade education." These are the six questions:

1. What is the first thing that comes to your mind when you hear the name "Abraham Lincoln?"
2. What is black colonization?
3. Was Abraham Lincoln good or bad for blacks in the 1860's?
4. Is Abraham Lincoln and what he stood for good or bad for blacks in 1974?
5. What is the Emancipation Proclamation?
6. What is your opinion of Abraham Lincoln?

Ms. Fulcher broke the responses down by some simple social classifications. Government officials, business executives, doctors, lawyers, and writers were classified as black professionals. Engineers, nurses, union leaders, school officials, and teachers were classified as higher white-collar workers. Firemen, policemen, social workers, secretaries, and soldiers were classified as lower white-collar workers. Dock workers, trash collectors, custodians, and assembly line workers were classified as wage or blue-collar workers. Another classification included the unemployed, welfare recipients, present and former convicts, and criminals. Mothers were considered a special classification as well, perhaps because of Ms. Fulcher's own reading of the importance of mothers in light of the history of the black family. The elderly were given a category to themselves, as were students.

The tabulated results of the survey, broken down according to these categories, appear below:

Professionals

	#1	#2	#3	#4	#5	#6
Pro-Lincoln	3	4	4	3	4	4
Anti-Lincoln	12	10	13	14	13	13
Neutral	2	3	0	0	0	0

Higher White-Collar

	#1	#2	#3	#4	#5	#6
Pro-Lincoln	9	3	5	5	6	6
Anti-Lincoln	10	13	13	12	13	13
Neutral	0	3	1	2	0	0

Lower White-Collar

	#1	#2	#3	#4	#5	#6
Pro-Lincoln	16	16	17	17	17	17
Anti-Lincoln	4	3	4	3	4	4
Neutral	1	2	0	1	0	0

Blue-Collar

	#1	#2	#3	#4	#5	#6
				Question		
Pro-Lincoln	3	1	2	3	3	3
Anti-Lincoln	8	8	9	8	8	8
Neutral	0	2	0	0	0	0

Unemployed

	#1	#2	#3	#4	#5	#6
				Question		
Pro-Lincoln	2	1	2	2	2	2
Anti-Lincoln	6	6	6	6	6	6
Neutral	0	1	0	0	0	0

Mothers

	#1	#2	#3	#4	#5	#6
				Question		
Pro-Lincoln	3	1	1	1	1	1
Anti-Lincoln	0	2	2	2	2	2
Neutral	0	0	0	0	0	0

Elderly

	#1	#2	#3	#4	#5	#6
				Question		
Pro-Lincoln	2	2	2	2	0	2
Anti-Lincoln	0	0	0	0	2	0
Neutral	0	0	0	0	0	0

Students

	#1	#2	#3	#4	#5	#6
				Question		
Pro-Lincoln	4	3	5	5	5	5
Anti-Lincoln	21	20	20	20	21	20
Neutral	1	3	1	1	0	1

Summary of Survey

	PRO-LINCOLN	ANTI-LINCOLN	TOTAL
PROFESSIONALS	4	13	17
HIGHER WHITE-COLLAR	6	13	19
LOWER WHITE-COLLAR	17	4	21
BLUE-COLLAR	3	8	11
UNEMPLOYED	2	6	8
MOTHERS	1	2	3
ELDERLY	2	0	2
STUDENTS	6*	20	26
TOTAL	41	66	107

*Includes one neutral.

Ms. Fulcher provided an analysis of the figures and provided percentages which make the survey even more startling. Three-fourths of the black professionals are anti-Lincoln. Almost seventy percent of the higher white-collar workers are anti-Lincoln. Three-fourths of the black unemployed are anti-Lincoln. Two-thirds of the black mothers are less than enthusiastic about Lincoln. Almost eighty percent of black students are anti-Lincoln, and that figure, of course, practically guarantees that future surveys will not see these figures turned around for some time to come. Almost three-fourths of blue-collar workers are anti-Lincoln. Only the elderly and lower white-collar workers retain the respect black soldier Edgar Dinsmore predicted would be Lincoln's forever. All the elderly interviewed and eighty-one percent of the lower white-collar workers are pro-Lincoln.

Among black professionals, knowledge of Lincoln's activity in behalf of colonization is high. In fact, their opinions almost perfectly reproduce the opinions of black professional Frederick Douglass one hundred years ago. They feel that Lincoln freed the slaves too slowly and that he did so only to save the Union, but they do realize that, in the context of the 1860's, Lincoln's policies certainly helped blacks. The minority opinion among black professionals is well represented by historian Benjamin Quarles, author of *Lincoln and the Negro*, still the definitive treatment of that subject in the field of Lincolniana. Quarles feels that Lincoln moved as fast in behalf of the slaves as public opinion would permit.

Opinions among the higher white-collar workers are similar to those among professionals, and this is important, for the group includes the teachers who will shape future opinions on Lincoln. The thirty-two percent of higher white-collar workers who are pro-Lincoln are an interesting group. They know about colonization, too, but they interpret it as Lincoln's efforts to lead blacks to self-help in a congenial atmosphere. They also feel that Lincoln wanted freedom for all, black and white.

The rest of the groups seem less aware of colonization. Blue-collar workers and the unemployed distrust Lincoln's motives for emancipation as "political." Although Ms. Fulcher does not say so, these groups seem to share with particular intensity the pervasive distrust of politics in American society in general. Incidentally, the minority in these groups who are pro-Lincoln are *very* pro-Lincoln and consider him a savior who alone stood between blacks and a continuing slave status for many years to come.

Black mothers seem to blame Lincoln for the plight of the freedman after emancipation. Black students, like black professionals and higher white-collar workers, are anti-Lincoln because Lincoln, they say, used freedom as a means to the end of saving the Union.

Those groups which are pro-Lincoln seem to be as aware of the facts of Lincoln's career as those that are anti-Lincoln. They merely interpret the facts differently. The elderly, for example, are aware that the Emancipation Proclamation did not free all the slaves, but they trust Lincoln's way of going about freeing the slaves.

Lower white-collar workers see all the difference in the world between legal freedom and legal slavery, and therefore they enthusiastically admire Lincoln as the bringer of freedom. They dismiss Lincoln's interest in colonization because it was always a voluntary rather than forced colonization which he envisioned. The only dissenters in this group dislike Lincoln because the Emancipation Proclamation itself did not actually free all the slaves and because freedmen were left in a poor condition.

There are encouraging signs for Lincoln's reputation even in this rather dismal reading of the current barometer of opinion. Most encouraging to anyone interested in history is the rather high level of information among people not selected, apparently, on a basis of interest in history. Thirty years ago, even ten or twenty years ago, knowledge of the practical effectiveness of the Emancipation Proclamation, of Lincoln's interest in colonization, or of his letter to Horace Greeley explaining his policies as a function of his duty to save the Union were considered fine points, subtleties which were well known in the profession but which were unknown to the man in the street. Blacks probably have a higher awareness of such things than whites today because these things are absolutely central to their history and because their history has become a major area of emphasis in all public education. Whatever the case, all historians and students of history should rejoice to see that they have not been talking simply to each other, and that things that were professional subtleties yesterday are today's common knowledge.

In regard to Lincoln's views on race and his policies concerning slavery, the fundamental pieces of evidence have not changed since Frederick Douglass's day, but popular opinion has changed in many ways. The results of a survey taken years hence might be quite different. Among historians, the sensational anti-Lincoln arguments of the late 1960's are clearly taking a new turn, and this survey proves that these changes in opinion become widespread in time.

CUMULATIVE BIBLIOGRAPHY 1974 - 1975

Selections approved by a Bibliography Committee consisting of the following members: Dr. Kenneth A. Bernard, Belmont Arms, 51 Belmont St., Apt. C-2, South Easton, Mass.; Arnold Gates, 289 New Hyde Park Rd., Garden City, N.Y.; Carl Haverlin, 8619 Louise Avenue, Northridge, California; James T. Hickey, Illinois State Historical Library, Old State Capitol, Springfield, Illinois; E. B. (Pete) Long, 607 S. 15th St., Laramie, Wyoming; Ralph G. Newman, 18 E. Chestnut St., Chicago, Illinois; Hon. Fred Schwengel, 200 Maryland Avenue, N.E., Washington, D.C.; Dr. Wayne C. Temple, 1121 S. 4th Street Court, Springfield, Illinois. New items available for consideration may be sent to the above persons, or the Lincoln National Life Foundation.

1974

ARMSTRONG, WILLIAM H. 1974-25

The Education of/Abraham Lincoln/by William H. Armstrong/Coward, McCann & Geoghegan, Inc./New York/ [Copyright 1974 by William H. Armstrong. All rights reserved.]

Book, cloth, 8⅛" x 6⅛", fr., 127 (1) pp., illus., price, $4.64.
Juvenile literature

BROWNE, RAY B. 1974-26

Lincoln-Lore/Lincoln/in the/Popular Mind/edited/by/Ray B. Browne/with/a/foreward/by/Russel B. Nye/(Device)/Popular Press/Bowling Green, Ohio 43403/ [Copyright 1974 by The Bowling Green University Popular Press, Ray B. Browne, Editor.]

Book, cloth, 9¼" x 6¼", xiv p., 3-510 pp., illus., price, $20.00

CARTER III, SAMUEL 1974-27

The Riddle/Of/Dr. Mudd/By Samuel Carter III/(Device)/G. P. Putnam's Sons/New York/ [Copyright 1974 by Samuel Carter III. All rights reserved.]

Book, cloth, 8½" x 5½", 380 pp., maps on inside of front and back covers, illus., price, $8.95

COOLIDGE, OLIVIA 1974-28

Olivia Coolidge/(Device)/The Apprenticeship of/Abraham Lincoln/Charles Scribner's Sons/New York/ [Copyright 1974 by Olivia Coolidge. All rights reserved.]

Book, cloth, 8¼" x 6¼", viii p., 242 pp., illus., price, $6.95
Juvenile literature

JONES, ALFRED HAWORTH 1974-29

Alfred Haworth Jones/Roosevelt's/Image/Brokers/Poets, Playwrights, and the/Use of the Lincoln Symbol/National University Publications/Kennikat Press . 1974/Port Washington, N.Y. . London/ [Copyright 1974 by Alfred Haworth Jones. All rights reserved.]

Book, cloth, 8¼" x 5¾", 134 (6) pp., price, $8.95

LINCOLN MEMORIAL UNIVERSITY 1974-30

Lincoln Memorial University Press/(Device)/Fall, 1974/ Vol. 76, No. 3/Lincoln Herald/A Magazine devoted to historical/research in the field of Lincolniana and/the Civil War, and to the promotion/of Lincoln Ideals in American/Education./[Harrogate, Tenn.]

Pamphlet, flexible boards, 10⅞" x 7⅞", 117-168 pp., illus., price per single issue, $1.50

LINCOLN MEMORIAL UNIVERSITY 1974-31

Lincoln Memorial University Press/(Device)/Winter, 1974/ Vol. 76, No. 4/Lincoln Herald/A Magazine devoted to historical/research in the field of Lincolniana and/the Civil War, and to the promotion/of Lincoln Ideals in American/Education./[Harrogate, Tenn.]

Pamphlet, flexible boards, 10⅞" x 7⅞", 169-228 pp., illus., price per single issue, $1.50

LONGFORD, LORD 1974-32

Great Lives/Abraham Lincoln/Lord Longford/Introduction by Elizabeth Longford/(Portrait of Lincoln and son)/Weidenfeld and Nicolson London/ [Copyright 1974 by George Weidenfeld and Nicolson Limited and Book Club Associates. All rights reserved.]

Book, cloth, 10" x 6½", fr., 231 pp., scenes of Lincoln-Douglas debates on inside front and back covers, illus., price, $8.50. British edition.

SORMANI, LUCA 1974-33

Lincoln/E Il Razzismo/Dopo La Schiavitu/(Device)/Edizioni Cremonese/Roma/ [Published February 10, 1974 by Edizioni Cremonese, Roma. Copyright 1973 by Edizioni Cremonese, Roma. Entire contents of book printed in Italian language.]

Book, paperback, 7¼" x 6⅛", 138 pp., price, $2.50.

1975

ILLINOIS STATE HISTORICAL LIBRARY 1975-1

Illinois/History/Volume 28/Number 5/February 1975/Abraham Lincoln/Down the Mississippi to New/Orleans—East-Central Illinois/Connections—Defeat Brings/Victory—River Traffic versus/Rail Traffic—Assassination/Attempts—"Leather Lungs" for/Lincoln—Views of the British/Press—The Summer White/House—Problems of the First/Lady—Ominous Dreams—Those/Who Stayed Away—The Coffin/Conspiracy—Lincoln and the/Press—Historic Indian Canes/(Portrait of Lincoln)/A Young Mr. Lincoln/(Cover title)/ [Copyright 1975 by the Illinois State Historical Society. Published by the Illinois State Historical Library for the Illinois State Historical Society, Old State Capitol, Springfield, Illinois 62706.]

Pamphlet, flexible boards, 10" x 7¾", pages 99-119, illus., price, 20¢.

ILL. STATE HISTORICAL SOCIETY 1975-2

Journal/of the Illinois State Historical Society/Volume LXVIII/Number 1/February 1975/Contents/3 Introduction/William K. Alderfer/9 Lincoln and Frederick Douglass: Another Debate/Christopher N. Breiseth/27 Lincoln and the Politics of Morality/Ronald D. Rietveld/45 Lincoln and the Weight of Responsibility/Don E. Fehrenbacher/57 Lincoln and Congress: Why Not Congress and Lincoln?/Harold M. Hyman/74 Lincolniana: Lincoln and the Printmakers/Harold Holzer/85 Book Reviews/96 Picture Credits/Cover: Statue erected in 1909 in the courthouse square of Lincoln's birthplace, Hodgenville, Kentucky./ Sculpture by Alexander Weinman./Copyright, Illinois State Historical Society, 1975 (Device) 14 Printed by Authority of the State of Illinois/(Abraham Lincoln Issue)/

Book, flexible boards, 9¾" x 7¾", 95 (1) pp., illus., price, $2.00

(LINCOLN MEMORIAL SHRINE, THE) 1975-3

A Selective Bibliography/Of/Books, Phamphlets (sic), Letters, Documents/And Other Materials/In/The Lincoln Memorial Shrine/(Picture of the shrine)/Redlands, California/1975/(Cover title)/

Pamphlet, paper, 8½" x 5½", 39 (1) pp., illus. (Contains a brief history of the shrine and a selective bibliography of their collections of books, pamphlets, manuscripts, art objects, photographs, stamps, coins, artifacts and periodicals.)

LINCOLN MEMORIAL UNIVERSITY (1975)-4

The Abraham Lincoln Library and Museum/(Embossed portrait of Lincoln and lettering)/that government/of the people,/by the people,/for the people,/shall not perish/from the earth/(Cover title)/

Pamphlet, flexible boards, 11" x 8½", 16 pp., illus. (Contains historical data on the formation and growth of Lincoln Memorial University, data and illustrations of its Lincoln collection along with an illustrated picture of its future goal, the construction of a new memorial, The Abraham Lincoln Library and Museum, to house its collection.)

Douglass on Lincoln

'Faith was strained, but it never failed'

Frederick Douglass, born a slave on Maryland's Eastern Shore, escaped to freedom and became one of the great Americans of the 19th century. In these remarks, delivered in Washington April 14, 1876, Douglass placed in historical perspective similar American statesman Abraham Lincoln. The text was edited by Thomas Curtis, a Baltimore lawyer and author of "Retrieval from Civil Rights."

DOUGLASS

Honor Frederick Douglass With a Coin

To the Editor:

The year 1995 will mark the 100th anniversary of the death of Frederick Douglass, and many hope a circulating coin will be issued to honor him. Douglass is best known as an abolitionist writer and editor, a former slave (who freed himself). Through his lecture tours of England, he roused sympathy and support for the anti-slavery cause, and some historians credit him with keeping England from openly declaring its support for the Confederacy during the Civil War.

Douglass published and wrote The North Star, the widely read abolitionist newspaper, while living in Rochester. He supported John Brown's cause to help free the slaves and later urged the enlistment of black soldiers in the war to preserve the Union.

In later life, Douglass served as a Federal marshal, United States minister to Haiti, statesman and tireless worker for civil rights. He sought to get African-Americans the right to vote, then helped organize that vote against the forces of racism and bigotry. Douglass became a symbol of a people's struggle to be free.

Martin Kozlowski

A commemorative dollar coin bearing Douglass's image would honor him and give impetus to those who still seek to uplift the human spirit. The coin would affirm the image and reality of America as a true multicultural society — not just a blend of cultures, but a society that can celebrate its diversity.   GERALD MUHL
Rochester, Sept. 7, 1994

Editorial Notebook

A Supreme Court Exhibition

With Clarence Thomas As Frederick Douglass

The hype surrounding "Strange Justice," the new book that castigates Clarence Thomas and the Senate committee that confirmed him, has obscured an interesting development: Mr. Thomas's campaign to bypass his critics by appealing directly to what he seems to view as his natural constituency, the conservative black middle class. The campaign has been conducted mainly below radar, through private receptions like the one in Chicago for a former welfare mother who put several children through college.

But late last month, Mr. Thomas convened a more public gathering of 35 African-Americans, including same from the black press, for three hours of off-the-record meetings at the Supreme Court. The guests were plucked from the Rolodex of the Washington talk-show host Armstrong Williams, one of Justice Thomas's closest friends. Mr. Williams invited a select few to a special meeting in the Justice's chambers. The Thomas camp asserts that race had nothing to do with who was invited to the meetings. Given what transpired, that is difficult to believe.

A few things stand out. First the gathering drew at least implicitly on the belief among many African-Americans that Mr. Thomas's treatment by the press was at least partly a consequence of his race, as Mr. Thomas himself claimed three years ago when he called the confirmation hearings a "high-tech lynching." Second, the visitors greeted Mr. Thomas with a standing ovation, and the Justice spent much more time than was planned shaking hands, much like a candidate on the stump. He defended his jurisprudence with winning personal anecdote and folksy aphorism.

The meeting generated much-needed warmth for a man whose isolation has been thorough and emotionally difficult. Most important, perhaps, is that a lengthy session of questions went by without so much as a breath about Anita Hill. Mr. Thomas alluded to the troubles only obliquely, when he remarked emphatically that African-Americans ought never to "tear each other down." The Hill affair, then, was the pink elephant in the corner that

everyone tried not to see. The deference was understandable, given how the guests were chosen and that nearly all were visiting the Court for the first time. Still, even crusty Washington veterans were charmed. Said one left-leaning woman, a Democratic Congressional aide: "I was deeply impressed. He was so warm, so human. He really cares about blacks."

Mr. Thomas's trump card turned out to be his art. Hanging from his chamber walls were several portraits, among them: the great abolitionist Frederick Douglass; W.E.B. DuBois, co-founder in 1905 of the Niagara Movement, which later became the N.A.A.C.P.; and a runaway slave, entitled "Running for Freedom." Mr. Thomas's art seemed to reassure those who had worried about the hostility toward civil rights he displayed as chairman of the Equal Employment Opportunity Commission under Ronald Reagan. Here instead was the Court's most radically conservative Justice draped in the mantle of Frederick Douglass.

How can this be? Douglass pressed Abraham Lincoln relentlessly to declare war on the South for the sole purpose of ending slavery. With the official end of slavery, Douglass pressed just as relentlessly for Federal protections of the new and fragile freedom. Is it conceivable that the great abolitionist would embrace a Justice who opposes virtually all Federal rights protections and derides them as "special treatment"?

As a former slave, Douglass had a special aversion to brutality. How would he feel about a Supreme Court Justice who has twice argued in dissent that the Eighth Amendment's prohibition of cruel and unusual punishment should not apply to the treatment of prison inmates, even when they are gratuitously and viciously beaten.

There may be a plausible line of argument that transforms Frederick Douglass into the Clarence Thomas we've seen so far. If so, Mr. Thomas should lay it out. Meanwhile, visitors to the Court need to be less taken in by the trappings of power, and more intent on the brutal character of Mr. Thomas's justice. *BRENT STAPLES*

NYT 11/13/94

LIFELINE

A QUICK READ ON WHAT PEOPLE ARE TALKING ABOUT

HAVE PACHYDERM, WILL TRAVEL: Tai the elephant has landed safely. The 8,000-pound tusked one was overnighted Tuesday via Federal Express from Los Angeles to Orlando to shoot scenes today for an upcoming Disney movie, *Dumbo Drop.* "Everything went flawlessly," says FedEx's Shirlee Finley. "She got first-class service, as did her trainer." And how much did it cost to ship the hefty gal to make her deadline? "We're not at liberty to divulge our contractual arrangements, but let's just say we didn't take an overnight letter and multiply it by 8,000 pounds."

LOVE SONG: Just in time for Valentine's Day, Columbia Records will release a Julio Iglesias and Dolly Parton duet. *When You Tell Me That You Love Me* is the third release from Iglesias' new album *Crazy,* which also includes collaborations with Sting, Art Garfunkel, Dave Koz and the London Symphony Orchestra.

LET FREEDOM RING: The Smithsonian is celebrating Black History Month by honoring one of America's foremost statesmen, Frederick Douglass. *Majestic in His Wrath: The Life of Frederick Douglass,* at the National Portrait Gallery in Washington, D.C. Friday-Nov. 19, commemorates the 100th anniversary of the death of the orator and abolitionist. The exhibit includes more than 80 paintings, sculptures, photographs and documents depicting his birth into slavery in 1818 to his fight against post-Civil War racism. Highlights: papers granting Douglass his freedom in 1846, and the letter he wrote to President Lincoln outlining his plan to help slaves escape to the North.

National Portrait Gallery
DOUGLASS: Honored with Smithsonian exhibition

UNSUNNY DAYS: The Sunshine State may have lost some its shine for

Smithsonian Puts on Douglass Exhibit

National Portrait Gallery

The life of the abolitionist and civil rights crusader Frederick Douglass is commemorated on the 100th anniversary of his death with an exhibition at the Smithsonian's National Portrait Gallery, in Washington. The show, "Majestic in His Wrath: The Life of Frederick Douglass," will run through Nov. 10.

More than 80 paintings, sculptures, photographs, engravings and documents, along with personal memorabilia, will trace Douglass's life from his birth into slavery in about 1818 through the years following his escape to the North in 1838, when he began his lifelong struggle for the abolition of slavery and for full equality for African-Americans.

Among the notable documents on view are the papers granting Douglass's freedom in late 1846, Douglass's letter to President Lincoln, dated Aug. 29, 1864, outlining a plan to undermine the Confederate cause by encouraging slaves to escape to the North, and a letter asking a member of the Rochester Ladies Anti-Slavery Society for $2.50 to help a runaway slave flee to Canada.

The exhibition also contains Douglass's 1817 edition of "The Columbian Orator," the book that fired his ambition to become a public speaker and introduced him to antislavery thought.

Lectures, storytelling programs and tours have been scheduled in conjunction with the exhibition. A film series featuring the lives of such noted African-Americans as Harriet Tubman, Sojourner Truth and Douglass will run through April 23. The National Portrait Gallery, Eighth and F Streets, N.W., is open daily from 10 A.M. to 5:30 P.M. Admission is free. Reservations for lectures, tours and films can be made by calling (202) 357-2920. For museum information, call (202) 357-1300.

'My Bondage and My Freedom' Douglass' best known work

Q. – I have the book *My Bondage and My Freedom* by Frederick Douglass, with an introduction by Dr. James McCune Smith, published in New York and Auburn, by Miller, Orton & Mulligan, 1855. It is in fair condition with some stain spots. I would like to know its value and where I might find a buyer. – R.W., Palestine, Ohio.

ANTIQUARIAN BOOKS
by Bob and Anne Hayman

A. – Frederick Douglass, the famous abolitionist, writer and orator, was one of the important black leaders for much of the 19th century. He was born in Maine in 1817, the son of a slave and a white father, originally named Frederick Augustus Washington Bailey.

At the age of 10 he was sent to Baltimore to live with a relative of his owner and it was during this period that he learned to read and write. In 1838 he escaped to New Bedford, Mass., married and changed his name to Frederick Douglass.

His first published work was *Narrative of the Life of Frederick Douglass, an American Slave*, which appeared in 1845 in Boston.

Second and third editions were published there in 1846 and 1847. The book created so much publicity for Douglass that, fearing he would be reenslaved, he fled to England. While there his friends raised enough money for him to return to America and buy his freedom.

Back in this country, he quickly established himself as the foremost spokesman for the black race. One authority says in this respect that Douglass was the prototype for men like Martin Luther King Jr., who was not to appear for another 100 years. During the 1840s and '50s Douglass was active as a lecturer in the abolitionist cause.

The Douglass book you have, *My Bondage and My Freedom* (New York & Auburn, 1855), is not his most valuable book but it is possibly his best known one. We find two recent retail prices for your book, one of $100, the other $85. Neither of these copies is in what could be called very good condition so the exact value of your copy depends on just what condition it is in. You have described your copy as "fair with some stain spots," which indicates to us that it is in less than very good condition.

The value of your book is in great contrast to that of Douglass' first book mentioned above. The latter is valued in the $1,000 range and the Ahearns price it somewhat higher than that. Of course, the Ahearns say that

their estimated values are believed to be accurate plus or minus 20 percent. In that light, perhaps their estimate of $1,500 is not as outlandish as it seems.

Your book was also reissued in 1881 in a revised and enlarged edition under the title *Life and Times of Frederick Douglass, Written by Himself*. It is available at fairly low prices in the 1881 and later editions, possibly in the range of $25 or so.

As to where you might sell your copy, any dealer in used books would probably be interested, depending on its condition. Of course, since he will have the task of selling it he cannot pay anything even approaching its retail value.

* * * * *

The Mini Page

© 1989 by Universal Press Syndicate

By BETTY DEBNAM

Frederick Douglass' Secret

Frederick Douglass was born in February 1818 in Maryland. His mother was a slave. He never knew his father. He also never knew his exact birthdate. He died on Feb. 20, 1895, at the age of 77.

Douglass' first wife was Anna Murray. She was a free black. She sold her belongings to help Douglass escape from Baltimore to freedom in New York City. They had been married for 44 years when she died in 1882.

Douglass helped recruit blacks like the ones shown above for the Union forces. He also helped slaves escape to freedom through the Underground Railroad.

A young black slave who lived a long time ago had a secret.

The slave's name was Frederick Bailey. He lived in Baltimore, Md.

The secret was that he could read.

A very understanding mistress had taught him his ABCs.

His mistress was proud of her bright student. She told her husband how well he was doing.

Frederick's owner became very angry. He made his wife stop giving Frederick lessons and would not let him have books.

Most slave owners would not let their slaves learn to read. It was thought that if slaves learned this skill, they would be harder to handle.

Frederick kept his secret . . . but didn't stop learning.

He became more determined than ever.

He would trick his white playmates into letting him see their homework.

Frederick Douglass was active in the Republican Party. He was appointed U.S. marshal for the District of Columbia. This was the top law job in the district.

He later bought a book, "The Columbian Orator." An orator is a good speaker. He studied the book to learn how to make good speeches. The book also gave him other ideas. Many of the speeches were about freedom.

At the age of 20, Frederick ran away to freedom. He changed his name to Frederick Douglass in order to escape capture by slave catchers.

Learning to read had changed his life. He grew up to be an outstanding black leader against slavery. He became an important author, newspaper editor and speaker.

He also spoke out against alcohol abuse and in favor of women's rights and black rights.

The Mini Page wishes to thank the National Park Service and the Frederick Douglass National Historic Site for help with this story.

The Inside Story
Inner-views with the body parts

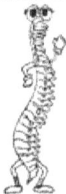

I am your spine:
- I am also called your backbone.
- I protect a cord of nerve tissue called the spinal cord. It is very fragile. It runs up your back and carries messages to your brain from all parts of your body
- I have a row of 33 bones called vertebrae (VERT-eh-bray) Each of these bones has a hole in it. These holes line up to make a tube. The spinal cord passes through this tube. It is protected by the bones of your spine.
- I also help you bend. Because of me you can move your head from side to side. You can bend backward and forward, and twist from side to side.
- I can bend because I am made up of so many separate bones.
- A soft material (cartilage) keeps the bones of your spine from rubbing together. There is a layer of it between each one of your 33 vertebra bones.

The Mini Page thanks Children's Hospital National Medical Center for help with this series

---

Fun with reading
by B. Literate

NEWSPAPERS CAN HELP YOU LEARN TO READ

For parents and kids to enjoy together

Literate people are good readers who use what they learn by reading to lead a happier, more successful life

The words in the first two rows begin with the letter Y. What sound do you hear?

B. Literate

yolk   you   young   yield

yogurt   yarn   yellow   yum

Which picture does not begin with the Y sound?

HEY

Here's how to make the big and little Y. Practice here

Aa Bb Cc Dd Ee Ff Gg Hh Ii Jj Kk Ll Mm
Nn Oo Pp Qq Rr Ss Tt Uu Vv Ww Xx (Yy) Zz

Buzz through your newspaper and The Mini Page for pictures and words beginning with the letter Y

Mini Spy . . .

Mini Spy and her friends are on a toboggan, having winter fun. See if you can find

- dolphin
- flower
- candy cane
- frog
- number 3
- acorn
- seal
- word MINI
- snake
- evergreen tree
- doll head
- heart
- fish

BASSET BROWN THE NEWS HOUND'S

TRY 'N FIND

Words that remind us of Frederick Douglass are hidden in the block below. See if you can find LEADER, WRITER, ADVISER, ORATOR, HERO, CEDAR HILL, WASHINGTON, CIVIL WAR, DOUGLASS, EQUAL, BAILEY, NEWSPAPER, RIGHTS, SPEAKER, FREEDOM, SLAVERY, JUSTICE, AUTHOR, BLACK, READER, EDITOR

LET'S LEARN ABOUT FREDERICK DOUGLASS

```
S P E A K E R I G H T S V W C
F S I U B N E W S P A P E R E
R L U T I B A I L E Y I D I D
E A S H A A D V I S E R I T A
E V T O C L E A D E R H I E R
D E I R K O R A T O R E O R H
O R C I V I L W A R X R R V I
M Y E D O U G L A S S O P M I
W A S H I N G T O N S L A C J
```

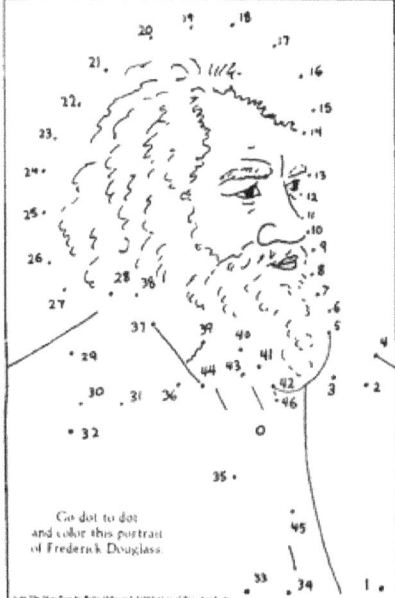

Go dot to dot
and color this portrait
of Frederick Douglass.

Rookie Cookie's Recipe
Chili

You'll need:
- 2 tablespoons vegetable oil
- 1 onion, chopped
- 1 pound ground beef
- 1 can tomato soup
- 1 15-ounce can tomato sauce
- 1 teaspoon chili powder
- 1 cup tomato juice

What to do:
1. Place oil and onion in a large skillet. Cook over medium heat until onion is tender.
2. Add beef. Cook until brown. Drain.
3. Stir in tomato soup, tomato sauce, chili powder and tomato juice.
4. Turn heat to low and simmer for 1½ hours. Stir occasionally. Serves 4.

Meet Myleka

Myleka grew up wanting to be a singer. Now her dream has come true. She released her first album last year.

Myleka, 17, grew up in New Jersey. She used to sing along to records by her favorite singers, Natalie Cole and Diana Ross.

Her father saw she had talent and took her to a music teacher.

She began performing at age 8. She sang in talent contests, at charity events and on TV.

Her career really took off when she won a big talent contest in New York City.

The Mini Page — Teacher's Guide

For use by teachers and parents at home and at school.

For use with issue: Frederick Douglass' Secret

Main Idea: This issue is about the life and home of Frederick Douglass. The following is a list of activities to be used with this issue. They are listed in order of difficulty, with the easier procedures coming to hand first. Ask the children to do the following:

1. What pieces of furniture do you see in the photos of Frederick Douglass' home? How is it different from the way your home is decorated?

2. Why is Frederick Douglass such a hero to Blacks? What do you think it would have been like growing up Black in the 1800s? How have conditions changed for Blacks? Who are some black heroes of long ago and today? Which black hero do you admire most? Why?

3. Many people have had stamps designed to honor them. Create a Frederick Douglass stamp.

4. Find the following words: equal, civil, memorial, orator, parlor, action, separate, editor, conduct, capitols, proper, equipped. Define and make up a new sentence for each one.

5. Create a Black History Month poster. What are some other ways to celebrate the month and honor Black heroes?

6. Pretend you are a tour guide of Cedar Hill. Make up a speech to give the tourists about Frederick Douglass and his home.

7. Look through your paper about articles on famous blacks. Also look for articles about blacks who are good role models.

8. Discuss reasons for a black person whom you admire.

Mighty Funny's Mini Jokes

WHAT IS THE DIFFERENCE BETWEEN A NEW PENNY AND AN OLD DIME?

NINE CENTS

THAT'S MIGHTY FUNNY

Q: Where do cows go for lunch?
Mighty Funny: The calf-ateria.

Q: What kind of tree grows on your hand?
Mighty Funny: A palm tree.
(All sent in by Giselle de Freitas.)

Let's Visit the Frederick Douglass Home

Frederick Douglass

When Frederick Douglass moved to Washington, D.C., he was 54 years old and very famous. The fight against slavery had been won.

The Civil War was over. There was still much to do. Douglass continued his work for equal rights for blacks. Douglass was a well-to-do man. In 1877, he bought a 14-room home that sat on 14 acres of land. It was called Cedar Hill.

Today, many school children visit his home, Cedar Hill. It is a beautiful home, high on a hill overlooking Washington, D.C. Park rangers, like the one on the far left, sometimes dress in clothes similar to those worn in the 1800s.

This is a photograph of Douglass at work at his desk in his library. He wrote books, newspaper articles and speeches. He also kept accurate business records.

Douglass' second wife was Helen Pitts, a white woman. They were married for 11 years before he died. After his death, she worked to keep his home, Cedar Hill, as a memorial to him. Today, the home has 90 percent of his original furniture.

Cedar Hill is run by the National Park Service. Park rangers conduct tours and care for the property. There is also a visitors center that shows a film about Douglass' life.

The gentleman's guest bedroom. Douglass lived in what is called the Victorian Age, named after Queen Victoria of England. People were very proper. Husbands and wives sometimes did not share the same bedroom when they visited. They slept in separate rooms.

The East Parlor was more formal. It was here that Douglass received important visitors.

The West Parlor was less formal. Douglass relaxed here with his family. He had two daughters, three sons and 21 grandchildren.

The Douglass family entertained many famous guests at dinner.

The kitchen was very well-equipped. Coal or wood could be burned in the stove.

"I was an ex-slave...and yet I was to meet the most exalted person in this great republic..."

Sojourner Truth (1797? -1883) lacked many of Douglass' opportunities, working as a field hand and never learning to read or write. Intense religious experiences, in which she heard God's voice, gave her unusual independence and strength. Despite her illiteracy, she was, like Douglass, a skillful public speaker, and was recognized as a religious leader as early as the 1830s. In 1843 she turned her attention to abolitionism, and in 1850 she began demanding equality for women as well.

Sojourner Truth

Since the mid-1850s Sojourner Truth had been living in Battle Creek, Michigan, and during the war she worked there to raise money for black soldiers. In 1864 she was inspired to make the cross-country trip to Washington so that she could meet the president. After the meeting she dictated a letter to Rowland Johnson describing her experience. She directed him to arrange for it to be published in the *National Anti-Slavery Standard* (December 17, 1864). Although she had had to wait outside Lincoln's office for three and a half hours before he could see her, her letter betrays no annoyance at the inconvenience. "I had quite a pleasant time waiting until he was disengaged, and enjoyed his conversation with others: he showed as much kindness and consideration to the colored persons as to the white — if there was any difference, more. ... The president was seated at his desk ... [After I was introduced,] he then arose, gave me his hand, made a bow, and said, 'I am pleased to see you' ... I must say, and I am proud to say, that I never was treated by any one with more kindness and cordiality than were shown to me by that great and good man, Abraham Lincoln, by the grace of God President of the United States for four years more. He took my little book, and with the same hand that signed the death warrant of slavery, he wrote as follows: 'For Aunty Sojourner Truth, Oct. 29, 1864 A. Lincoln.' As I was taking my leave, he arose and took my hand, and said he would be pleased to have me call again. I felt that I was in the presence of a friend."

Frederick Douglass

In the spring and summer of 1863 Douglass had been recruiting black soldiers for the army, but by August he was discouraged by the way black soldiers were being treated. (They received less pay than white soldiers, they could not become officers, and they risked being sold into slavery if captured by the Confederates.) Some of Douglass' friends convinced him to take his concerns to the president. In his autobiography, *Life and Times of Frederick Douglass*, 1882, he describes the meeting: "I need not say that at the time I undertook this mission it required much more nerve than a similar one would require now. ... I was an ex-slave, identified with a despised race; and yet I was to meet the most exalted person in this great republic. ... Happily for me, there was no vain pomp and ceremony about [Lincoln]. I was never more quickly or more completely put at ease in the presence of a great man, than in that of Abraham Lincoln.... As I approached and was introduced to him, he rose and extended his hand, and bade me welcome. I at once felt myself in the presence of an honest man — one whom I could love, honor and trust without reserve or doubt. Proceeding to tell him who I was, and what I was doing, he promptly, but kindly, stopped me, saying 'I know who you are, Mr Douglass; Mr. Seward has told me all about you. Sit down, I am glad to see you.' ... He impressed me with the solid gravity of his character, by his silent listening not less than by his earnest reply to my words. Though I was not entirely satisfied with his views, I was so well satisfied with the man and with the educating tendency of the conflict, I determined to go on with the recruiting."

www.ingramcontent.com/pod-product-compliance
Lightning Source LLC
Chambersburg PA
CBHW021429090426
42739CB00009B/1413